Epitácio Pessoa

Epitácio Pessoa
Brazil
Michael Streeter

HAUS HISTORIES

First published in Great Britain in 2010 by
Haus Publishing Ltd
70 Cadogan Place
London SW1X 9AH
www.hauspublishing.com

A CIP catalogue record for this book
is available from the British Library

ISBN 978-1-905791-86-6

Series design by Susan Buchanan
Typeset in Sabon by MacGuru Ltd
Printed in Dubai by Oriental Press
Map by Martin Lubikowski, ML Design, London

Contents

Epitácio Pessoa (1865–1942).

Preface

The journey had begun in high spirits and with great hopes. The *Curvelo* set sail from Brazil on 2 January 1919 with former government minister and judge Epitácio Pessoa on board. His destination was Paris, where he was to serve as the head of his country's delegation to the historic Peace Conference convened to deal with the aftermath of the First World War. As the ship slipped out of harbour the mood was upbeat, not least because this was a rare chance for Brazil to play a role on the world stage. As one of the belligerent powers on the victorious Allied side it had been rewarded with the right to have three full delegates at the Conference – more than most of the other countries attending.

By late January, however, the mood on board the *Curvelo* had turned to one of frustration and irritation. The sluggish vessel had chugged so slowly across the Atlantic that the Conference's opening ceremonies on 18 January had come and gone with the greater part of the Brazilian delegation literally all at sea. There was a certain irony about this particular ship hampering the progress of Pessoa and his team, one that was not lost on those on board. In her previous life the *Curvelo* had been known as the *Bremen* and was one of more than 40

German ships the Brazilians had confiscated during the war. It was the ownership of those ships that was one of the two most pressing issues that the Brazilian delegation hoped to resolve at the Conference – if they ever got there. In a way, the other matter involved German ships also – it concerned the fate of a large consignment of Brazilian coffee that had been trapped in German ports at the outbreak of the war back in 1914.

As the *Curvelo* limped slowly into Lisbon harbour, the final stretch of the journey nearly in sight, Pessoa could have been forgiven for thinking the worst was over. But in the Portuguese capital the head of the Brazilian delegation heard the tragic news that their country's president Francisco de Paula Rodrigues Alves had died. It was true he had been ill for some time, so his death came as no great surprise. But the loss of a genuinely popular head of state on the eve of such an important conference was still a blow to morale. As the *Curvelo* finally brought Pessoa and his entourage into French waters on 28 January, it may even have seemed as if their diplomatic mission was jinxed. Neither he nor his fellow delegates could know that, on the contrary, the fortunes of both the delegation and more especially Pessoa himself were about to take a dramatic turn for the better.

Acknowledgements

The author would like to thank Professor Linda Lewin for her help and encouragement in the research for this book.

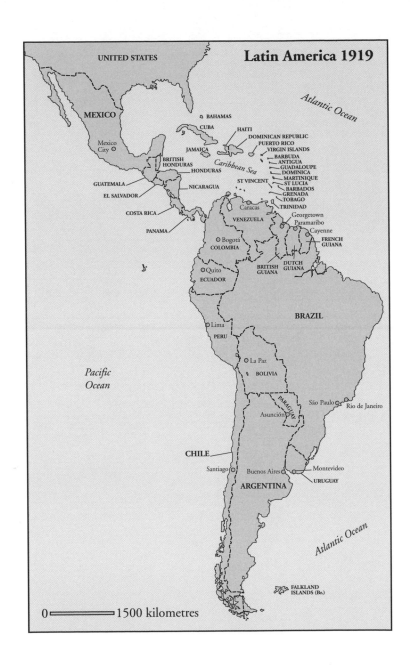

Latin America 1919

UNITED STATES

Atlantic Ocean

MEXICO

Mexico City ⊙

BAHAMAS
CUBA
HAITI
DOMINICAN REPUBLIC
PUERTO RICO
VIRGIN ISLANDS
JAMAICA
BARBUDA
ANTIGUA
GUADALOUPE
DOMINICA
MARTINIQUE
ST VINCENT — ST LUCIA
BARBADOS
GRENADA
TOBAGO
TRINIDAD

Caribbean Sea

BRITISH HONDURAS
HONDURAS
GUATEMALA
EL SALVADOR
NICARAGUA
COSTA RICA
PANAMA

Caracas ⊙
VENEZUELA

Georgetown
Paramaribo
Cayenne
FRENCH GUIANA

Bogotá ⊙
COLOMBIA

BRITISH GUIANA
DUTCH GUIANA

Quito ⊙
ECUADOR

BRAZIL

Lima ⊙
PERU

La Paz ⊙
BOLIVIA

Pacific Ocean

São Paulo ⊙ ⊙ Rio de Janeiro

PARAGUAY
Asunción ⊙

CHILE

Santiago ⊙
Buenos Aires ⊙ ⊙ Montevideo
URUGUAY

ARGENTINA

Atlantic Ocean

FALKLAND ISLANDS (Br.)

0 ▭▭▭ 1500 kilometres

I
The Life and the Land

1

Creation of the Republic: 1889–1900

Ever since Portuguese sailors landed there at the start of the 16th century, Brazil has been stuck – one might say burdened – with the label of a country of the future. It is not hard to see what attracted those Europeans and why it was felt the country offered so much potential. The coastline provided an easy supply of the valued brazilwood (hence the country's subsequent name) a tropical climate, natural harbours and an abundance of wildlife. In more modern times the country's fertile soils have produced sugar, rubber, coffee and most recently ethanol, while underground and off the coast considerable reserves of oil and natural gas have now been discovered.

The raw, physical statistics of Brazil never cease to amaze. Jutting out into the Atlantic Ocean towards Africa, it occupies some 8.5 million square kilometres or more than 3.2 million square miles, making it the fifth largest country on Earth. Its vast 4,600-mile coastline runs from French Guiana in the north to Uruguay in the south and on land it has boundaries with ten other countries. Only two South American countries, Ecuador and Chile, do not share a frontier with Brazil. Then there is the mighty Amazon river, the world's largest river in terms of volume. More controversially, Brazilian experts now claim it as the world's longest river too, eclipsing the Nile. The country's population is also impressive in scale, standing at around 190 million by 2009.

Yet on the eve of the 'modern' era of Brazil, which started in the final decade of the 19th century, this South American colossus seemed as far as ever from fulfilling the potential that had so long been predicted for it. Its contacts were largely with Europe where this former Portuguese colony – it became independent in 1822 – was seen, notably by the British, as a useful source of basic raw materials, a destination for poor immigrants and worthy of some modest investment but little else. In return the Brazilian elite looked to Europe for much of their intellectual, cultural and political inspiration. The United States, the dominant force in the Western hemisphere but self-absorbed with its westward expansion after the horrors of its Civil War, paid Brazil little serious attention. Even some of Brazil's South American neighbours had relatively little to do with this large but underpopulated country of 14.3 million people on their doorstep.

The reasons the country had such a minor role on the world stage at this time were partly geographic, partly cultural. Brazil was the only Portuguese-speaking colony in South America and this fact alone has always set it apart from its mostly Spanish-speaking neighbours. Under the famous Treaty of Tordesillas of 1494 Spain and Portugal had carved up the world to determine which of them would control any new lands they discovered. The only portion of South America that lay on Portugal's side of this line was the then-unknown Brazil. Another difference was that Brazil remained a monarchy long after the former Spanish colonies

THE PEOPLES OF BRAZIL
When the Portuguese first began arriving in Brazil in the early 16th century there was a sizeable indigenous population of perhaps around three million. However, in such a vast country the Amerindians were scattered relatively thinly. One group of peoples is known collectively as the Tupí-Guaraní, who between them occupied points all along the Brazilian coast and the Amazon river. Another group is known as the Tapuya. Some anthropologists prefer to classify the indigenous peoples of the country according to the terrain they lived in and the lifestyle this afforded them. The two main groups were divided between those living in tropical forests, who survived by agriculture and fishing, and those living on the plains and more arid areas, who hunted, fished and gathered their food. However they are classified one thing is clear: the Amerindians suffered enormously from the arrival of the colonists, through disease, loss of land and enforced labour. As for the settlers, many initially marvelled at the simplicity and apparent innocence of the native inhabitants' lives. The Portuguese also learnt from them; for example, how to grow new crops such as manioc. Though the colonists tried to put the Amerindian population to work on plantations, they were generally regarded as unsuitable, a factor that ultimately led to the importation of African slaves. Thus a third racial group arrived in the country, to go with the white Europeans and original inhabitants. Out of these sprang a mixed-race people, initially the product of white men and Amerindian women, known as *cabolos*, while later the mix became one between Africans, Amerindians and whites. In the late 19th and early 20th century it was generally accepted in Brazil that the whiter a person was the 'better', and it was also widely believed that society itself was 'whitening'. In 1890 whites made up an estimated 44 per cent of the population.

had become independent republics in the first half of the 19th century. Moreover, nature had conspired to further isolate Brazil from its neighbours, not just by the Amazon jungle but the river systems of both the Amazon in the north and the Paraguay-Paraná-Plata rivers to the south. Its closest relations – and rivalries – were with Uruguay, Paraguay and Argentina to the south. Finally, the winds and currents of the

Atlantic Ocean made it easier to sail between Europe and Brazil than between Brazil and the United States, something that remained a significant factor until the era of sail gave way to that of steam.

Two key social and political events at the end of the 1880s combined with a series of economic and cultural changes to start the process of modernising Brazil, and helped put an end to its insular stance. The first of these events was the abolition of slavery in 1888. This was followed the next year by the toppling of Pedro II and the establishment of a republican system of government. Meanwhile the growth of the coffee industry, which was already expanding, inevitably involved the country in more dealings with the US, where consumers had developed a real taste for Brazilian coffee beans. With slavery abolished, the coffee growers of São Paulo state – an increasingly powerful group in the country – also needed fresh sources of labour. Much of this came via immigration, which had already been growing since the middle of the century. Another important development, and one which would become a major factor in Brazilian politics for decades to come, was the rising influence of the military, and especially the army. Together these forces and others helped make the final decade of the 19th century one of the most tumultuous in Brazilian history.

ooooo

When slavery was finally abolished in 1888, it was the culmination of a process that had continued throughout the 19th century rather than a sudden act. An 1831 law that technically abolished the Brazilian slave trade was ignored and it was not until 1850 that the practice ended. Two decades later a law was passed to make free any children born to a slave woman after 1871. Many of the reasons for this gradual dismantling of slavery lay abroad. The British navy played a key role in the ending of the slave trade, its ships intercepting the slave ships that plied their trade between the Brazilian coast and Africa, and ultimately forcing the reluctant Brazilian authorities' hands in 1850. Meanwhile French intellectuals petitioned the Brazilian monarchy to abolish slavery completely. Yet there was a growing movement from inside Brazil too, from among those who simply saw slavery as immoral. This is unsurprising given that at this time intellectual circles in Brazil were hugely influenced by European and especially French and British thought.

A prominent home-grown abolitionist was Joaquim Nambuco, the well-dressed son of a planter from Pernambuco in the north-east of the country. The north-east, predominantly a sugar growing area, and one that was suffering economically even as the coffee industry to the south was growing, had traditionally relied on slave labour. In 1880 Nambuco wrote a manifesto for the Anti-Slavery Society in which he pointed out how slavery had helped undermine the country's international status. 'Brazil does not want to be a nation morally isolated, a leper, expelled from the world community,' he wrote. At the same time there was a practical, modernising school of thought which believed that in addition to moral concerns, there was an economic reason for abolishing slavery. Unless Brazil did so, the argument went, the country could not modernise its economy. Nambuco reflected this view, too, when he wrote that slavery 'prevents immigration, dishonours manual labour, delays the appearance of industries, promotes bankruptcy, diverts capital from its natural course, keeps away machines and arouses class hatred'. He also made clear in his autobiography just how much he and other Brazilians were influenced by Europe. 'We Brazilians ... belong to America on a new and fluctuating layer of our mind, while we belong to Europe on all the stratified levels. As soon as we acquire the least culture, the latter predominate over the former. Our imagination cannot fail to be European ... .'[1]

The final decree to end slavery in Brazil was signed on 13 May 1888, and was known as the Golden Law. This freed the remaining 750,000 or so slaves left in the country, though the fortunes of many of them certainly did not improve overnight. The scene was now set for the other major blow to old Brazil – the fall of the monarchy itself. Brazil was unique among the former European colonies in South America that won independence in the early 19th century by being a monarchy rather than a republic. The first ruler was the Portuguese Dom Pedro I, but after a military setback against Argentina and amid growing unhappiness at perceived Portuguese influence, he abdicated in 1831. His Brazilian-born son Pedro was just five at the time of his father's departure, and a regency was installed until 1840, when the boy was deemed fit to rule in his own right as Pedro II.

Pedro was by no means a disastrous ruler of Brazil. He led an exemplary private life and appears to have had few vices, save perhaps for an 'amorous friendship' by letter with a female correspondent. The Emperor oversaw the development of the country's judicial system and was well read; indeed he earned the title of 'philosopher-king', though he was certainly no intellectual. Pedro II also made a favourable impression with Americans when he visited the United States in 1876. This was one of the first concrete steps towards closer relations between the two countries, even if the monarch's main reason was to attend the US's centennial exhibition in Philadelphia. By all accounts the Americans were somewhat surprised to see that the ruler of exotic Brazil turned out to be tall, fair-haired and blue eyed, and that in matters of dress he favoured a sober suit. He was dubbed the 'Yankee Emperor' and praised for being an enlightened ruler.

Yet Pedro possessed no great vision for Brazil at a time when the country cried out for inspiring leadership. He presided over a very limited parliamentary form of government that saw a monotonous alternation of Conservative and Liberal administrations – factions too busy with their own internal squabbles to bring any vitality and drive of their own to govern the country. His government and these politicians largely represented the interests of the rural landowning elites, many of whom had supported slavery until not long before its abolition. Once slavery had gone, Pedro and his system were no longer seen as useful in protecting this elite's interests, and one of the main planks of support for the monarchy was removed. Indeed, the end of slavery and recent power squabbles between church and state are often cited as two of the principal reasons for the end of the monarchy. Yet the situation was more complex than that.

Brazil had for some time had its own republican movement, whose influence waxed and waned over the decades but which had a strong following among sections of the ever more powerful São Paulo province coffee elite. Their interests were far from selfless; they preferred a strongly regionalised system, under which they could run their industry as they saw fit, free from the heavy hand of central government. Then there was the role of the military, and especially the army, sections of which were heavily influenced by positivist philosophy and who favoured a strong but technocratic modern state. The influence of the military in Brazilian political life had been growing since the bloody if successful war against Paraguay which had ended in 1870, and which helped awaken nationalistic sentiment and dissatisfaction among junior ranks. (It also led to the death of up to half of Paraguay's entire population.) Though these two groups – the soldiers and the coffee growers – ultimately had different views on how the country should be run, they both came to agree that the monarchy was anachronistic and holding back the country's development.

On top of these powerful forces, personality was also involved. The Emperor was by now a sick man, suffering from diabetes. Indeed, it was his daughter Princess Isabel as heir presumptive who, in the absence of her father, with a gold pen encrusted with diamonds and emeralds, had signed the decree abolishing slavery – a cause which she personally backed, and which earned her lasting fame. (A politician at the time unhelpfully remarked that she had won the slavery debate but lost the throne – a prophetic comment.) Three times, in fact, she stood in to rule as regent due to her father's absence, making her the first woman to serve as a head of state in the Americas. Among the press and intellectual circles, however, there seems to have been little appetite for Isabel to take over on a permanent basis. This was largely due to the criticism – much of it unfair – aimed at her French husband, the Count d'Eu, grandson of King Louis Philippe of France.

When the monarchy did finally fall, it went with a whimper, amid a public mood that can almost be described as indifference. Throughout 1889 there had been increasing republican criticism of the monarchy and its latest government under chief minister Ouro Preto. Crucially, there were small but constant squabbles between the government and sections of the military. Finally, a leading figure in the army, Marshal Deodoro da Fonseca, was prevailed upon by colleagues to take action. Deodoro was a much-respected soldier and was also president of the recently-formed Clube Militar, a mouthpiece for military views – and of discontent. Though not in the best of health, the Marshal put aside his loyalty to Pedro and on 15 November the ailing soldier, on horseback, ordered troops to seize the War Ministry in Rio de Janeiro and surround the Royal Palace. In the confusion at the time it was unclear – and remains so – whether Deodoro's initial intention was to overthrow the entire monarchy or simply Ouro Preto's government. The outcome, however, was unambiguous. Within a few days Pedro who had not been in Rio at the time of the coup abdicated and was on his way into permanent exile. He died in a Parisian hotel two years later. Pedro's reported remark at the time of his ousting that 'this is my charter to freedom' reflects the pressures the Emperor had felt and perhaps helps explain why the monarchy collapsed so quickly and so peacefully. 'The nation received the Republic with stupefaction,' was the reaction of one observer.[2]

However, if the end of Brazil's monarchy was greeted with relative calm, the next decade was to prove anything but calm as the country struggled to come to terms with its new republican status. For though the end of the empire had long been foreseen, there was no off-the-shelf plan for what should replace it. One of the perennial problems of governing Brazil came from its sheer size. Coupled with its lack of internal communications systems, this made it hard to rule from the capital Rio de Janeiro. The country's provinces, which became known as states after the fall of the empire, were diverse, far-flung and often had conflicting interests. In the north-east were the old sugar states, once the powerhouse of the country's economy, and where during much of the 19th century people felt remote from the south of the country. Indeed it was not unknown for members of wealthy families in the north to travel to enjoy the cultural delights of Europe without ever bothering to journey down to Rio. By the last decade of the 19th century economic and thus political power had switched emphatically to the coffee-growing areas of the south, and chiefly the emerging state of São Paulo, plus the neighbouring mixed agricultural state of Minas Gerais. Further south still, and utterly remote from the north, was the gaucho, cattle-raising state of Rio Grande do Sul. Bordering on Uruguay and Argentina, this was a strategically important state which produced many of the nation's army officers. Reconciling such disparate areas in an overwhelmingly rural country was not easy. Another key factor in the political life of the First Republic was that political parties were state-based rather than national in scope, something that did not make reaching national consensus any easier.

The first task for the new regime was to fashion a new constitution, a document that was finally approved by a Constituent Assembly in 1891. It was consciously based on the US constitution, establishing a president and a two-chamber Congress. This at least helped to bring Brazil a little closer to Washington, where despite initial pleasure that Brazil had finally become a fellow republic, there was disquiet that Pedro II had been removed at the barrel of a gun. In effect Brazil had swapped a British-style constitutional monarchy for an American presidential system.

The key element of the new federalist Brazil was that it allowed considerable autonomy for the states to act as they wished. This was especially important for states such as

São Paulo, whose coffee elite saw themselves as the country's motor and who wanted to be able to dictate terms for growing and trading their valuable product. The resulting tensions between the president and the states, and the power struggles and alliances between the various states and their powerful elites, were to dominate Brazilian politics until the end of the First Republic. Other important measures included the separation of church and state, and the establishment of direct and universal suffrage, in other words the right to vote. However, as illiterates were specifically disbarred from voting and around 80 per cent of the population could not read or write, and as women were also denied the vote, most Brazilians were still excluded from any say in who governed them.

Deodoro was elected by members of the Assembly (which then became the Congress) to be the country's president in 1891 but his term did not last out the year. A proud and brave soldier from one of the country's best-known military families, he was ill-suited to the demands of political life. After falling out with and dissolving Congress, and faced with a potential naval revolt, he stood down in November. His replacement was Vice-President Floriano Peixoto, another respected soldier but an altogether colder and tougher politician than his predecessor – as his nickname of the 'Iron Marshal' suggests. For three years Floriano ruled the country essentially as a military dictatorship, presiding over a strong centralised government. Curiously, although his rule was against the spirit and intention of the constitution in his flouting of its attempts to encourage decentralisation, the new president was not initially opposed by the coffee elite. As businessmen the São Paulo republicans preferred order to chaos, and Floriano at least brought a measure of stability. Nonetheless, there were angry voices raised in Congress against the new president's high-handed intervention in state politics and his authoritarian approach. One of these voices belonged to a young lawyer named Epitácio Pessoa.

Epitácio Lindolfo da Silva Pessoa was born on an estate called Fazenda Prosperidade in Umbuzeiro in the state of Paraíba in the north east of Brazil on 23 May 1865. His parents Colonel José da Silva Pessoa and Henriquieta Barbosa de Lucena, who both came from well-connected families in neighbouring Pernambuco, had settled there a few years earlier. Neither Paraíba nor Pernambuco were large or powerful states, and by the time of Epitácio's birth the balance of power in the country had already switched to the large states in the south. Nonetheless the Fazenda property was a valuable livestock and sugarcane estate and both sides of the family had played a prominent role in Pernambuco politics. In particular Epitácio's maternal uncle Henrique was the governor of the state and would later be ennobled as the Baron of Lucena. Thus Epitácio, the youngest of five children, was born into a privileged and well-connected background. Yet the family's relative prosperity and position could not save it from one of the scourges of 19th century life – smallpox.

PARAÍBA STATE
One of the smaller Brazilian states, Paraíba became an important producer of sugar in Brazil along with neighbouring states in the north east of the country. Yet by the fall of the monarchy, Paraíba's economic importance had long since been eclipsed by the coffee growing states to the south. Separated from much of the rest of the country by geography and experiencing relatively little immigration in the late 19th century, it was a conservative state dominated by a small number of wealthy oligarchic cliques. Epitácio Pessoa was to become the head of one such family-based group.

It was during a trip to Recife in Pernambuco in 1874 that both Epitácio's parents contracted, and died from, the deadly disease. He was just eight years old at the time. The five children were farmed out to various members of the family, with Epitácio ending up living with his Aunt Marocas, the widow of his father's late brother Joaquim, in Recife. It was here that the boy received his education, though he did return to spend time at the family estate at Umbuseiro during the school holidays. Epitácio remained with his aunt until he finished his studies, which in his case and typically of the time meant enrolling at the city's prestigious law school.

At the end of the 19th century Brazil was sometimes accused of not producing enough scientists, engineers and agricultural experts to meet the need of a country looking to expand its economy and diversify into industry. One thing the country was very good at producing, however, was lawyers. At the time that Epitácio studied there, the law school in Recife was regarded as the country's leading academic institution and he was part of a golden generation of young men – the so-called generation of the Eighties – who would go on to play prominent parts in the future of the country – though not just as lawyers. One of his fellow students, for example, was Graça Aranha, whose 1902 work *Canaan* is regarded as the country's first real novel of ideas. Both men were also taught and influenced by one of their teachers, the renowned Tobias Barreto, a devotee of German philosophy. It was a typical elite Brazilian education of the time – dominated by European thought. The young Pessoa, however, was not eclipsed by the brilliant company he kept, and ultimately graduated near the top of his class in 1886. Partly this was because the youngster took his studies very seriously, preferring to stay with his adoptive family and work hard rather than staying in the racier student quarter. Yet there is no doubt, too, that he was exceptionally able and readily took to the law. It was a discipline and a subject which he would put to great use over the coming decades.

After graduating from Recife Pessoa spent a brief spell as a public prosecutor in nearby Cabo, a tough posting for a young lawyer. He did not stay there long, however, as he quickly found himself up against the local elites – a far from unusual occurrence in Brazilian states. In particular he clashed with a prominent judge thanks to his dogged determination to prosecute a murder case. In the end the able but inexperienced prosecutor resigned. Nonetheless it was a valuable lesson for Pessoa, who was already developing the toughness needed to thrive in the hard-nosed world of state and national politics. He then moved to Rio de Janeiro, arriving there in 1889 just two weeks before the creation of the Republic.

Thanks to his family connections Pessoa was given a ringside seat at the critical events leading up to and including the fall of the monarchy, a fortuitous but beneficial experience for any ambitious young man. His uncle, now the Baron of Lucena, was a friend of Deodoro da Fonseca, whom Pessoa met, the man poised to deal the fatal blow to the empire. Indeed, he joined his uncle in a meeting at Deodoro's home in Rio the very night before the Republic was proclaimed. Lucena went on to become Deodoro's *de facto* chief minister. Two other important though less prominent contacts were General Almeida Barreto, a member of Deodoro's staff, and Lieutenant João José Soares Neiva, Lucena's brother-in-law. Both men helped set up the young lawyer in public life. Neiva wanted his brother Venâncio to become governor of Paraíba and Barreto's actions as military commander there enabled this to happen. And the man chosen to be cabinet secretary to Venâncio, himself a graduate of the Recife law school, was Epitácio Pessoa. So just weeks after his arrival in Rio, he found himself aboard a ship heading back to Recife and life as cabinet secretary to the new governor of his home state.

Pessoa's rapid introduction to Brazilian politics did not end there. In 1890 the governor chose his cabinet secretary as one of his candidates for the election of the state's five local deputies to sit in the federal Constituent Assembly in Rio. This was the body that was to metamorphose into the chamber of deputies once the 1891 constitution was approved. Pessoa was duly elected, winning the largest number of votes of the five successful candidates. However, his career and many of those in his family and circle received a major setback when Deodoro quit as president, making way for the autocratic Floriano. The new hard man in charge of Brazil was quick to make his mark not just in Rio but across the country's states as well. Soon after Floriano took over, Venâncio Neiva was ordered to stand down to make way for one of the president's allies. He refused, and had to be forcibly removed from his offices. His young colleague Pessoa looked on in horror at the demise of Deodoro, the removal of his own state boss, and the way that the new president was toppling state governors across the land. As he put it at the time: *Side by side with one large coup d'etat there were twenty smaller ones.*[3]

Though his local sponsor had been deposed as governor, Pessoa remained a federal deputy and in January 1891 returned to Rio de Janeiro to take part in congressional debates. It was now that the immaculately turned-out deputy displayed an eloquence, mastery of the law and above all political courage that was to win him many admirers on the national political stage. He chose to use his maiden speech in the chamber to denounce the behaviour of the increasingly dictatorial Floriano and continued the attack in subsequent declarations too. In one speech the precocious young lawyer described his own speech as *one more cry of resistance and revolt against the daily attacks of the federal government against the autonomy of the states.* He openly criticised what he called the *violence committed daily in the name of legality* as well as the *disorganisation and anarchy reigning in all parts of the Republic; the autonomy of the states annihilated; the laws crushed at our feet; the State Assemblies dissolved.* And in one particularly powerful passage he declared: *Gentlemen, what have we seen since the Republic was restored to legality? We have seen repeating itself that scene which, sadly, we were so many times witness to in the time of the monarchy – the deposing of governors of provinces accompanied by the most fierce reaction, with one difference, however: this removal was then done by a competent power, and by a legal act, which is done now by the use of force and violence, and accompanied by the annihilation of all state powers, and more than this, is covered with the blood of the Brazilian people!*[4]

Pessoa had little or nothing to gain politically from these eloquent attacks, which stemmed from genuine conviction. Throughout his career he would advocate the importance of respecting legal principles and to his dying day he saw himself as a man of the law, both in his career and as a politician. It formed part of his self-image. However, such principles were not always easy to uphold in the often murky world of national and state politics in First Republic Brazil, and in the years ahead Pessoa would himself be accused of falling short of the high standards he himself championed.

> ... the deposing of governors of provinces ... is done now by the use of force and violence ... covered with the blood of the Brazilian people!
> **EPITÁCIO PESSOA**

Pessoa was not the only critic of Floriano, and during 1892

a number of prominent military officers demanded that Floriano hold an election. The first name on the list was that of Almeida Barreto, Pessoa's contact. The Iron Marshal took special exception to shows of dissent from within the military, and later they and a number of civilian critics were arrested. The hapless opponents were then put aboard a ship and sent to what was Brazil's equivalent of Siberia – the Amazon jungle. Their personal circumstances were not quite as bad as might be imagined, however, as they were exiled to Manaus, then a fine city built on the proceeds of the booming rubber industry. Nonetheless, they were forced to stay in this remote part of Brazil, far from political influence, until the end of Floriano's rule.

Pessoa did not share the fate of Barreto and the others, though the reason for is not entirely clear. Observers at the time and later claimed that he was forced to flee to Paraíba in 1893 to escape arrest in Rio. In his home state he found refuge among local politicians opposed to the President. In 19th-century Brazil it was not hard to escape the authorities by heading for the many remote and sometimes lawless parts of the countryside. However, his daughter Laurita Pessoa, who wrote a lengthy biography of her father, denied that he had needed to escape, and argued that the Iron Marshal had spared him arrest because of his admiration for him. From what we know of Floriano, this seems unlikely. What we do know is that for a period, until after the fall of Floriano, Pessoa kept a low profile.

The Iron Marshal himself had more pressing problems to deal with. In 1893 a civil war broke out in Rio Grande do Sul, always a sensitive area because of its closeness to Argentina and its close ties with the Brazilian army. The fighting between Federalists and Republicans was based partly on ideology and local politics, and partly on personality and rival economic groups. The fighting was vicious too, with prisoners often having their throats cut. More of a direct challenge to Floriano was a naval revolt in Guanabara Bay off the capital Rio. The navy, which had had stronger links with the monarchy than the army, was envious of the army's prominent role in Brazilian political life. In September 1893 Admiral Custódio de Melo turned those grievances into action when he took command of Brazil's fleet and threatened to bombard the capital if Floriano did not resign. The President stayed characteristically firm, however, and was helped also by the intervention of the US Navy. Its warships sailed into the harbour to protect American shipping, and this had the probably unintended effect of breaking the Brazilian navy's blockade. The revolt ended in 1894.

Floriano's rule had shown that central government could exert a measure of control over the country, fulfilling the first part of the new republic's distinctly positivist motto 'Ordem e Progresso' or 'Order and Progress'. Progress, however, was another matter. Though he had his supporters, including ultra-nationalists known as '*Jacobinos*', or Jacobins as well as much of the army, and though he had co-operated with sections of the São Paulo coffee elites, he lacked the broad power base to impose his own candidate to succeed him when his term of office expired. The candidate proposed by the Paulistas was Prudente de Morais from São Paulo, a politician whom Floriano apparently disliked. Yet, short of staging another coup, there was little the Iron Marshal could do to stop this transfer of power to the republic's first civilian president. Having lent their support to Floriano, São Paulo's coffee barons now had what they wanted – their own man in Rio. A disgruntled Floriano ostentatiously stayed away from his successor's inauguration ceremony, preferring instead to tend his roses. He died the following year.

The elections of de Morais in 1894 and that of his successor Campos Sales four years later were the start of a new era in Brazilian political life. It was sometimes called the '*café com leite*' or 'coffee with milk' period. São Paulo naturally represented coffee, while the powerful cattle-producing state of Minas Gerais was the milk. The colourful description oversimplifies the situation. In time other states, particularly Rio Grande do Sul, played an increasingly important role in national politics. And elected presidents could – and sometimes did – act against the narrow interests of those they supposedly represented. There is no denying, however, that these two states did drive national politics. This was particularly true of São Paulo – thanks to the central importance of coffee to the Brazilian economy.

Coffee production in Brazil rose massively at the start of the First Republic, from a modest 5.5 million 60kg bags in 1891 to 16.3 million a decade later. Reasons for this huge expansion in supply included the fertile land and suitable climate that southern Brazil possessed, a growing access to credit, cheap labour from immigration, and the lure of the great profits to be made. On the demand side, Americans had developed a taste for Brazilian coffee and were willing and able to pay for it. By 1901 the country was exporting 888,000 tonnes of coffee, making it Brazil's major source of export income, ahead of rubber. Yet there were risks involved. Coffee growing was not only labour-intensive and needed plenty of land, but it also took six years for coffee trees to start yielding fully. This made the industry slow to adapt to changing cycles of world demand, resulting in over-production. Meanwhile the republic had inherited a considerable budget deficit from the monarchy and did not help matters by fuelling its own speculative bubble by reducing credit controls in the first days of the provisional government. The state of the economy became so bad that in 1898 President-Elect Campos Sales himself sailed to London to meet the country's creditors and financiers to stem off potential bankruptcy. Here he struck a deal with the London bank Rothschilds, which had helped finance Brazil since her independence, to keep the country afloat.

The country's new civilian administration had other headaches, too, in the shape of major threats to law and order from the lower echelons of society in some of Brazil's most remote rural areas. The worst of these was at Canudos in Bahia state. Here, on a remote desolate abandoned estate deep in the *sertão* or 'backlands', a previously nomadic religious ascetic known as Antônio Conselheiro established a community. This was as far from the 'order and progress' of the Brazilian republic and the European culture of much of its elite as one could get. Canudos represented a parallel world of the lowly and dispossessed, people who felt threatened by the secular state and the end of monarchy, and who wanted to escape the clutches of rapacious landowners and officialdom.

Until 1896 this fluctuating community of up to 30,000 people had lived in relative peace and isolation, though occasional reports of its mysterious existence filtered through to Rio. Then a seemingly minor dispute over timber with a nearby town escalated into armed conflict. In quick succession three military expeditions marched from the coast, only for each to be humiliatingly defeated by the community's determined defenders. The third expedition numbered 1,300 men with artillery but its commanding officer was killed amid the slaughter. What had started out as a relatively minor skirmish was now seen as a full-blown challenge to the authority of the state. Many in Rio saw this as nothing short of a battle between the forces of civilisation and those of backward barbarism. Others feared it was part of an attempt to restore the monarchy. Finally a large contingent of 8,000 well-armed troops was sent in April 1897 to lay siege to the remote settlement. Still the 5,000 die-hard backlanders refused to surrender. Eventually, in October 1897, they were overwhelmed by the superior firepower and bayonets of the soldiers in a brutal denouement. Those who survived the attack were later executed.

Ever since the downfall of Canudos there has been much debate about the true nature of the community and its clash with authority. Some later saw it as a peasant rebellion and part of a larger class struggle, fuelled by the decline in the north-east's once important sugar industry and a surplus of labour in the coffee fields. At the time however it was simply seen as a threat to the integrity of Brazil's new republic. It was indicative, too, of how despite the end of slavery and monarchy, Brazil still had far to go along the path of modernisation. The fact that Brazil was still largely absorbed with its own internal affairs – such as Canudos – was shown by its reaction to the First Peace Conference in The Hague in 1899. This prestigious international gathering was held to discuss and codify issues such as the conduct of war, peace and war crimes, and just two Latin America countries were chosen to attend: Brazil and Mexico. But only the latter attended. Brazil declined the invitation on the grounds that it felt no subject of national interest would be discussed at the conference. Such insular views, however, were about to change.

2
Order and Progress: 1900–10

After his short but turbulent period as a deputy and his discreet flight from Floriano, Pessoa had returned to Rio de Janeiro by 1894. For a while he stayed out of public life and started up his own successful private law practice in the capital. The conventionally handsome 29-year-old bachelor – who was always immaculately dressed and for much of his life sported a moustache – also turned his mind to more personal matters, and in 1894 married Francisca Justiniana das Chagas, the 18-year-old daughter of a politician from Minas Gerais state. As was common practice at the time, he decided to go travelling with his new bride, and sailed off to spend a year in Europe, the traditional destination of many honeymooners from elite families. Their happiness seemed complete when Francisca became pregnant.

His joy was short-lived, however. Francisca died in childbirth in Paris on 24 April 1895 and their son was stillborn. It was a deep blow for the lawyer, who had already suffered the loss of both parents when he was just a child. Pessoa caught a ship back to Brazil taking with him the bodies of his young wife and son for burial. The tragedy of the event was compounded by the fact that in the following months and years he was dogged by gossip over the fate of his late wife's dowry. The implication was that he had tried to keep it. In fact, he offered to hand back the dowry to his parents-in-law.

Back in Brazil earlier than planned, Pessoa once more returned to his law practice, though he went back to Europe from March to November 1897. The tragic occurrence in Paris had not entirely dampened the lawyer's enthusiasm for Europe; indeed he would regularly return there in the years to come for both personal and professional reasons. Then, more than three years after the death of Francisca, he married again, on 8 November 1898, and once more to a woman from outside his own state. Her name was Maria da Conceição Manso Sayão – often known as Mary – and unlike his first wife she was the daughter not of a prominent politician, but of a well-known ear, nose and throat specialist from Rio de Janeiro. They were to have three daughters.

If Pessoa's private life had undergone a transformation towards the end of the century, so too did his career. Having spent four years in private practice, the lawyer was catapulted back into public life in 1898 when the new president Campos Sales chose him to be his Minister of Justice. Though he was still only 33, he was well-qualified for the post. Not only was he accepted as one of the more able lawyers of his generation, and an expert on boundary disputes, but the shrewd Pessoa also had a network of family and personal connections across Brazilian society and politics, which meant he understood how government worked. And though he was not formally engaged in political life from 1894 to 1898, he was heavily involved behind the scenes with the internal politics of his native Paraíba. Moreover, he had already caught the eye of the new president at the start of the decade when they had both served on a congressional committee. In particular Campos Sales, then a senator, was impressed with the young man's 'great juridical competence'.[1]

Once installed in the Justice Ministry, Pessoa set about preparing Brazil's civil code, a long-overdue addition to the Republic, in his usual thorough and methodical manner. At the time the country still operated under the terms of its old Portuguese-based civil code, one of the vestiges of colonial days. This task was to prove a lengthy one, but Pessoa began the process in 1899 when he commissioned Clóvis Bevilá-qua, a professor of civil law at Recife law school, to draw up new civil laws for the country. The first draft was ready that same year, though it would still take the best part of two decades for it to come into law. At the same time Pessoa did not neglect events back in Paraíba, where his network of personal ties and allies were forming what was rapidly becoming a political power base for him and his family. One revealing letter to a friend at this time shows both his skills as a politician, and his desire to further his own and his allies' interests in the state. Referring to a change in governorship, Pessoa wrote that it *offers the opportunity for a rapprochement with the state government. Continuing as I expect in the Ministry, I will, little by little, move to assume an influential position in the affairs of state so as to guarantee and maintain our party's rights.*[2]

> **Continuing as I expect in the Ministry, I will, little by little, move to assume an influential position in the affairs of state so as to guarantee and maintain our party's rights.**
>
> **EPITÁCIO PESSOA**

Inevitably, his continuing close interest in his state's politics laid him open to charges that he was abusing his position and his relationship with Campos Sales to further his own political ends in Paraíba. The president himself was an exponent of what became known as the 'politics of the governors'. He scrutinised the list of candidates in states' federal elections – and was the ultimate arbiter of who won such polls. His aim was to ensure that the deputies a state sent to the federal congress closely reflected that area's dominant political faction. By doing this, his intention was to remove factional disputes within states – and at the same time strengthen presidential power. Some Brazilian historians have since claimed this policy greatly increased the power of state-based oligarchies and hampered the development of national political parties in Brazil. In certain cases Campos Sales and his successors were prepared to step in and remove a governor's list of candidates and replace them with another – a process known as a *degola* or 'beheading'. This happened in Paraíba in 1900 after internal state squabbling led to the bizarre spectacle of two rival groups of local deputies turning up in Rio demanding to be recognised as Paraíba's legitimate elected representatives. Before that 'beheading' occurred, Pessoa was attacked in Congress over suspicions that he was guiding the President's hand to influence events in his home state. The precise turn of events is murky, but it seems there may have been some basis in fact for the claims.

In 1901, however, Pessoa was forced to leave office, though not because of alleged abuse of power. As Minister of Justice he also had responsibility for education and some of his reforms had angered students in the capital. The demonstrations grew during 1901 and Campos Sales felt obliged to act to quell the situation. The Minister of Justice offered his resignation, which was duly accepted. However, this was not a major fall from grace for Pessoa, who had simply been a convenient public scapegoat for Campos Sales. In January

1902 Pessoa was rewarded for his loyalty by being appointed a justice of the Supreme Court, and in June he was made Attorney General, a post he carried out simultaneously with that of judge for three years until October 1905. Then, under the presidency of Rodrigues Alves, friction with the Justice Minister J J Seabra, another Recife law school graduate, caused him to quit and concentrate on his role in the Supreme Court.

It was during this period that Pessoa cemented his reputation as an expert on international law and especially on border disputes, both national and international. In 1909, for example, he was asked by the then foreign minister to draw up a code of international public law, and in 1911 he was the Brazilian delegate to the International Commission of Jurists on the Codification of International Law. This held its first conference in Rio the following year. He was also asked to help out the Foreign Ministry with legal background on boundary disputes that Brazil had with its neighbours, including Peru. This was a time of a new coherence and assertiveness in foreign policy by Brazil, a clear break with the passive policy of the past. Much of this was due to the efforts and personality of the Foreign Minister himself.

José Maria da Silva Paranhos Jr, or the Baron do Rio Branco as he became, was made foreign minister in 1902 and served in the post until his death in 1912. He was an ideal choice, thanks partly to his upbringing and early career. His father had been a chief minister in the days of the empire and the new baron was well-educated, interested in Brazilian history and had also worked as a diplomat for many years. In particular he had worked as a Brazilian consul in Liverpool, where he had become fluent in English, and later headed a two-year diplomatic mission in Washington where he made important contacts. As a result of that mission, Rio

Branco became something of a national hero – his task in the US was to plead his country's case on a boundary dispute over the Misiones region with its great rival Argentina. The chosen arbitrator was US President Grover Cleveland. When the American head of state came down on the side of Brazil, Rio Branco shot from obscurity to celebrity status. In 1900 Rio Branco was asked to help in another boundary dispute, this time between Brazil and France over the Amapá area of French Guiana. After scouring the libraries of Europe to bolster his arguments, the Baron presented his country's case. The chosen arbiter this time was the Swiss president and he awarded the 101,000 square miles of land to Brazil. In two disputes Rio Branco had succeeded in significantly expanding Brazilian territory – without going to war.

When in 1902 the then president-elect Francisco de Paula Rodrigues Alves invited Rio Branco to return to take charge of Itamaraty – as the Foreign Ministry was known – it was therefore a popular choice. Although the diplomat was hesitant at first – the Baron was wary of the political intrigues in Rio de Janeiro that he could largely escape in overseas postings – the new president appealed to his sense of duty and patriotism and Rio Branco finally accepted the post. Indeed, so seriously did the Foreign Minister take his new position that he installed a bed in his office and often slept there when working late.

Rio Branco immediately set about improving and strengthening Brazil's image abroad, and by the time he died in office Brazil was represented in 39 countries around the globe. He made Joaquim Nabuco the first Brazilian Ambassador in Washington, a shrewd and successful appointment. One of Rio Branco's priorities was not just to improve his country's image but to reposition it diplomatically. Though he had a deep personal liking for continental Europe – though apparently not for Britain despite, or perhaps because of, his time there – the Baron realised that Brazil's future lay in the family of nations of the Americas. So his policy was to try to assert Brazil's position as the dominant country in South America while at the same time cultivating closer links with the United States. This policy is sometimes described as one of 'approximation'. It marked the start of a gradual transition for Brazil away from its traditional political and economic ties with Britain and Europe, and a move towards Washington.

Rio Branco's desire for a closer understanding with the US stemmed not from uncritical admiration – though he did respect the country and its people – but from national self-interest. The US was Brazil's main outlet for coffee and Rio Branco was determined to ensure that diplomacy supported his country's economic priorities. Rio Branco was also a supporter of the Monroe Doctrine – or at least the Brazilian view of it – which he credited with allowing Latin American nations to develop freely without outside interference. It did not mean, however, that Brazil slavishly followed the line pursued by the US, a country whose interest in Latin American affairs waxed and waned and which was often insensitive to its southern neighbours' points of view. For example, in 1909 Rio Branco complained to the US State Department over the aggressive way it had treated Chile over the matter of a US mining company there. This was an example of the careful balancing act he tried to conduct between trying to lead South America while at the same time keeping the US on its side. For its part, the US rarely felt the need or inclination to forge a special relationship with Brazil, a failing that often irritated the authorities in Rio.

Naturally enough, Brazil's twin policies of South American

pre-eminence and North American friendship did not always go down well with its neighbours, notably Argentina, which historically viewed itself as the leading country in South America. Inevitably, relations between the two nations fluctuated considerably and could be upset by seemingly trivial matters. For example, one of the warmer periods of relations between the neighbours was rudely if briefly interrupted in 1910 when the Argentine public decided that Brazil had not paid enough attention or respect to Buenos Aires' centennial celebrations. The Brazilian flag was publicly burnt in Argentina, prompting retaliatory protests in Rio de Janeiro. Rio Branco himself intervened to help calm the crowds. Yet though a public champion of good relations with other nations in South America, including Argentina, Rio Branco did not always seem to have much respect for them privately.

THE MONROE DOCTRINE
This famous doctrine was outlined by President James Monroe in 1823 and was essentially a 'hands off' warning to the European powers not to meddle in America's backyard – the Americas – and interfere with the newly independent nations there. Traditionally most Latin American nations viewed the doctrine with unease or mistrust, fearing that it really amounted to US hegemony in the region. Brazil however welcomed it – but chose to look upon it as a multilateral rather than unilateral US doctrine. This meant working together with the US and other leading nations in the Americas to ensure peace and co-operation.

On one occasion he told a US diplomat that 'no Spanish-speaking country is good and no person of Spanish blood can be believed'. On another he claimed that Argentina 'wishes to pose as a dictator' in South America.[3]

A good example of how Brazil's attitude towards the world had changed, but also how delicate a task it was maintaining good relations with both the north and south of the continent, came with the Second Hague Peace Conference in 1907. Brazil had declined an invitation to the first one in 1899 but now Rio Branco not only welcomed this second chance for Brazil to appear on a world stage, he also pushed the Americans to get his country preferential treatment. He succeeded to the extent of having the head of his delegation named as an honorary presidency of the conference. Brazil was the only Latin American country to be given this honour, despite Argentina's request for the same treatment. Its chief delegate was Rui Barbosa, a distinguished lawyer and well-known politician who had been the (less than successful) finance minister under the provisional government set up in 1889 and who had helped draft Brazil's new constitution. Yet another graduate of the Recife law school, he was a loquacious and persuasive speaker who still harboured ambitions to be president and who had gained a reputation as a firm opponent of military influence in politics.

The outcome of the Hague conference was mixed. Barbosa emerged as a hero among other Latin American delegations, helped by some rather unsympathetic US diplomacy. In a celebrated speech delivered in near-perfect French, he spoke of the 'great fortress' of sovereignty that all nations, however small, enjoyed – a sovereignty that was an 'equal right for all'. Such grandiose talk attracted the attention of Latin American public opinion, among whom his speech was interpreted as criticism of the bullying of bigger powers – notably the United States. Barbosa was described as the 'Eagle of the Hague' and given a hero's welcome when he returned to Brazil. The flip-side of the conference was that the apparent defiance of the US at The Hague undid much of Rio Branco's efforts at creating a more permanent and closer relationship with Washington. This was further undermined when Barbosa refused to attend a banquet in honour of visiting US naval officers at the end of 1907.

Brazilian nationalism and pro-US diplomacy were always uneasy bedfellows.

As we have seen, one of Brazil's key concerns was to ensure a healthy economic climate for its coffee, which accounted for much of its foreign export earnings, and this led to the dominance of the São Paulo coffee elites over Brazilian politics at the time. The benefits from the coffee industry were to prove doubly important as the country's short-lived rubber export boom – based on natural rubber cropped from the Amazon – was about to suffer a sudden, calamitous and permanent decline when faced with cultivated rubber plantations in Asia and falling world prices. Yet in the first decade of the 20th century coffee also had its problems. The potential for seemingly easy money in the industry had led to an enormous number of extra fields being devoted to coffee trees; in São Paulo state alone the number had rocketed from 220 million to 520 million between 1890 and 1900. The inevitable result was over-production, which in turn led to coffee surpluses and falling prices.

To rectify the problem, in 1902 the government banned the planting of new trees for five years, a moratorium that was later extended to 1912. Even this was not enough, however, as the 1906 harvest saw a record crop of 20 million sacks of beans. Three of the main states concerned by falling prices, chiefly São Paulo but also Minas Gerais and Rio de Janeiro state, put pressure on the national government to take further action. The outcome was the Taubaté Agreement of 1906 between the three states and the central government. Under its terms the states agreed to loan the national government money, while the executive agreed a policy to stockpile abundant coffee harvests when prices were low, and sell the produce on world markets when prices rose. This policy was known as valorisation. President Rodrigues Alves, a former governor of São Paulo who had succeeded Campos Sales in 1902, personally opposed the idea, but Congress saw differently, and the measure was formally adopted. An American diplomat in Rio observed: 'Never before has the country and especially everyone connected with the Government been so much under the influence of the coffee planters as at present and any measure which is seriously desired by that element is sure of immediate passage by Congress.'[4] By 1907 São Paulo alone was holding back eight million sacks. The policy continued until 1929.

A more open and professional foreign policy was not the only sign that Brazil was gradually becoming a more modern country. President Rodrigues Alves set his sights on improving the capital city itself. At his direction city engineers such as Pereira Passos began knocking down some of the less salubrious areas of the city to make way for new buildings and avenues, for example the Avenida Beira Mar. And while the city itself changed and started to resemble the tourist attraction it is today, the port too was modernised. Rio was becoming worthy of the new Brazil. Similar large scale building was underway in other cities too, while the new capital of Minas Gerais, built in the previous decade, was renamed Belo Horizonte in 1906.

The president was also keen to improve Rio's notorious image for poor sanitation and bad health. Public health expert Dr Osvaldo Cruz was brought in to help eradicate yellow fever, which was then prevalent in the city. By applying standard hygiene and social measures already in use elsewhere in Latin America, for example in Cuba, Dr Cruz's programme was highly successful, despite some initial local opposition from people who mistrusted any change. In 1903 a

THE LEGACY OF SLAVERY

The importation of slaves from Africa to Brazil began in the middle of the 16th century and continued until 1850 when the slave trade in Brazil was finally abolished. By then an estimated 3.5 million slaves had been brought to the country, a figure probably higher than the number of Amerindians at the time of the first white settlers. Some brought with them or developed their own trades as craftsmen but the majority worked in the fields. Initially a large number of Africans helped develop the sugar industry in the north-east, but during the 19th century they were largely responsible for the growth of the coffee industry further south. In this way slavery was widespread across much of Brazil, and not confined to just one part of the country. There were a number of slave revolts, the largest in the 19th century being in Bahia in 1835.

Slavery was finally outlawed in 1888 though by then a significant number of slaves had been manumitted. Even those who were freed, and even after abolition, the former slaves faced many difficulties. They had to compete with the new wave of largely white immigrants from Europe, whose labour was often preferred to the supposedly less hard-working inhabitants of African origin. A number of blacks became small landowners, while others headed to cities such as São Paulo in search of work. One legacy of slavery was that it brought not just racial but cultural diversity to Brazil, far more so than in many Spanish South American nations. It was even said that the country had the 'soul of Africa'. However, it was not until the 1930s that prominent thinkers in Brazil began to explore and embrace the country's rich African heritage.

total of 584 people died of yellow fever. By 1906 the figure had dropped to zero – after the disease had claimed 60,000 lives over the previous six decades. Now for the first time wealthy provincials seriously considered holidaying in Rio rather than Europe. However, Dr Cruz's campaign of vaccination to try to eradicate smallpox was less well-received. The introduction of large-scale vaccination into a culture for the first time has often met with fear and mistrust, and Rio was no exception. Various groups, including some ultra nationalists, whipped up opposition on the streets and in November 1904

rioting broke out. At one point a group of young army officers became involved and for a brief period there was armed
rebellion, though loyal army troops and naval recruits soon
restored order.

At this time Rio, in common with other cities such as São
Paulo, was home to a growing number of immigrants. This
was a period during which hundreds of thousands of economic migrants left the Old World of Europe and flocked
to the New World of the Americas in search of a new life or
in some cases the chance to earn money to take back home.
Brazil had long been an immigrant nation, from the Portuguese settlers in the early 16th century to the African slaves
imported to work the land when the self-sufficient and independent indigenous population were deemed unsuitable for
the task. A new wave of immigration began just before the
abolition of slavery, as plantation owners began to realise the
value of using immigrant labour. The figures tell the story:
between 1827 and 1930 a total of 3.8 million immigrants
came to Brazil, but the vast majority – 2.74 million – arrived
in the period from 1887 to the start of the First World War,
when European migration finally slowed.

The largest single group of migrants was Italians. They
made up around one-third of all immigrants from 1887 to
1930 and many of them went to work in the coffee fields.
By the end of the First World War Italians made up nearly
a tenth of the population of São Paulo state. However, they
were not the only European migrants; Spaniards, Portuguese,
British and French migrants came to the New World too. As
we shall see in the next chapter, there was also a significant
German immigrant population in the south of the country.
The main group of non-European immigrants were Japanese,
who began to arrive in significant numbers from around 1908

to work in the coffee plantations. Later many of them became small landowners.

Though most immigrants initially worked mostly in Brazil's overwhelmingly rural economy, they also had a huge impact on the size and demographic make up of the country's cities too. Here former slaves and others who had left the fields in search of work mingled with Italian craftsmen and migrants from the Middle East. The city of São Paulo experienced some of the most dramatic growth, expanding from a modest 64,000 inhabitants in 1890 to just under 580,000 by 1920. It was here that, thanks in part to the money associated with the coffee industry and the availability of labour, Brazil's fledgling industrial base began to grow. However, Rio de Janeiro remained by far the biggest city, its population rising from just over 550,000 at the start of the First Republic to 1.15 million by 1920.

Unsurprisingly, the fate of the immigrants was a mixed one. A significant number became landowners in their own right, others were artisans and craftsmen, while a few went on to become very successful businesspeople and industrialists. But many, too, returned home rather than put up with the low or even non-existent wages they received, the poor conditions in which they lived and the harsh treatment often meted out by bosses. In 1902 the Italian government even passed a law known as the Prinetti Decree that outlawed subsidised Italian immigration to Brazil, the result of numerous complaints by earlier emigrants about they way they were being treated. The following year more Italians left Brazil than arrived there. For some, dreams of a better life in the new world were to be cruelly shattered.

3

The Republic Unravels: 1910–17

By the end of the first decade of the 20th century Brazil was showing signs of becoming a more modern, outward-looking, prosperous and stable country. The coffee industry provided strong export earnings while the still-thriving rubber industry had yet to fall into its abrupt and terminal decline. After the early years of quasi-military rule, civilian presidents had presided over national politics, and a complex system had evolved in which the coffee states held the greatest power, but which also involved a network of inter-state and internal alliances, and social relationships. There were more visible signs of progress too, not least with the improvements made to Rio de Janeiro's streets, while the nation's railway network continued to expand.

Yet the years leading up to and including the start of the war in Europe were tough ones for the Brazilian republic. This was not helped by the choice of Marshal Hermes da Fonseca as the new president in 1910. The mere fact that he was a military candidate was enough to create disquiet in liberal and intellectual circles. Moreover Hermes, the nephew of the late Deodoro da Fonseca, was from Rio Grande do

Sul, a state growing ever more powerful under the guidance of Pinheiro Machado – at the time probably the most influential politician in the country. The new prominence of the southern state had begun to upset the delicate balancing act that existed between São Paulo and Minas Gerais over the previous decade. The alliance of Rio Grande do Sul with the elites of some of the other states, including smaller ones in the north, was also given an institutional voice with the creation of a national party – a rarity in Brazil in this period – the Conservative Republican Party or PRC. Significantly, the São Paulo state elite did not support Hermes for the presidency. Finally, there was the character and ability of Hermes himself. It would be wrong to suggest that Brazil's previous presidents had all been men of outstanding ability. Hermes, however, seemed especially ill-suited to lead his country at a time of growing unrest and discord. He was described by one renowned Brazilian historian as 'lacking political and administrative experience' and being 'kindly and indecisive'. The commentator added: 'He let himself be governed by circumstances, at the cost of public order and administrative achievements.'[1]

Hermes faced opposition even before he became president, as his election witnessed the first properly contested poll in the Republic's brief history. This does not mean it engaged much of the population; largely as a result of the country's ban on illiterates being able to vote, under half a million voters participated in the election, out of a total population of more than 20 million. Yet there was a mood of genuine excitement and contest when the veteran Rui Barbosa from Bahia state was nominated as Hermes' opponent, enjoying the important backing of the powerful republican party in São Paulo. Rui already enjoyed a special status in Brazilian society because of his performance at the second International Peace Conference. Now the politician once again lived up to his reputation as the 'Eagle of the Hague' as he toured the country, delighting large crowds with his powerful rhetoric and emotional style. In particular, he struck a chord with the country's emerging urban middle classes. It was the first time Brazil had seen this kind of populist electioneering style.

However, despite his popularity and the backing of São Paulo, Barbosa lost the election by more than 100,000 votes. It was always going to be a tough, perhaps impossible, task to win. The machinery of the state administration, controlled by the government, was against him. But Barbosa also suffered from not having a great track record himself in government and for his virulent attacks on the dangers of military influence in government. This criticism backfired as it united all military factions behind Hermes. It was a time when both the military and military issues were once more starting to play a more visible role in Brazilian life. Hermes had been appointed war minister in 1906 and his main goal was to try to modernise the country's army. In 1909 he was much influenced by a visit to Germany where he had observed at first hand the efficiency of the Kaiser's troops. By now many in Europe feared that war was imminent, and this mood of militarism struck a chord in distant Brazil too.

Though he had strongly opposed the quasi-military dictatorship of Floriano Peixoto, Pessoa had no objections to the election of Hermes da Fonseca. For one thing the two men were friends – Pessoa had known the family since he first came to Rio in 1889. He also knew he would need the authority of

> **The President of the Republic didn't contribute in any way to my return to political life.**
> EPITÁCIO PESSOA

the president to ensure he could increase his hold on and ultimate dominate the political scene in his native Paraíba. The lawyer's career as a Supreme Court judge had already been disrupted by illness. In March 1911 he was struck by a gall bladder disorder so serious that doctors advised he needed treatment in Europe to save his life. His gall bladder was removed in September of that year in Paris and the following month he returned to Brazil to resume his position at the court. However, less than a year later Pessoa resigned from the court for good. The stated reason for his departure was his health, but nonetheless he was well enough to be heavily involved in the politics of Paraíba and some opponents suggested the resignation was a ploy to allow him to return to frontline politics.

Many of Brazil's states were blighted by unrest at this time. Some of the disruption was caused by the direct intervention of groups of young military officers. Their aim was to remove what they considered to be self-interested, backward-looking conservative elites holding power in many states, which they were convinced were holding back the progress of the country. These so-called 'Salvationists' had some success in the north-east of the country. For example, they were able to oust the leaders in Pernambuco and Alagoas and impose their own governors. The Salvationists were loosely connected with President Hermes da Fonseca and generally opposed to the oligarchies supported by Pinheiro Machado. Both local and state politics became more complex, often depending on local personalities and grievances in difference regions. The disorder of these years underlined how fragile Brazil's republic was once the unofficial alliance between São Paulo and Minas Gerais – the 'coffee with milk' alliance – came under strain.

Amid such confusion Paraíba itself was threatened by a

private army of desperados and malcontents in the first half of 1912. According to one account, the town of Patos was reduced to 'one vast cemetery' by a group of 1,000 armed men. Fortunately the federal army, which had on other occasions supported Salvationist movements, stayed loyal and defeated them. Pessoa was credited with having helped save the state from attack by use of his 'skill in factional manoeuvring' and thanks to his personal relationship with President Hermes.[2]

The incident underlined both Pessoa's political skill and the extent of his connections at both state and national level. Soon he was able to formalise both. Despite his apparent ill health, the former Supreme Court judge was well enough in the autumn of 1912 to take a vacant seat in the Senate representing the state. There seems little doubt President Hermes cleared the way for this too. He took over the seat from an old friend from law school days, Castro Pinto, who had become the state's governor. Then, the following February, and again with the backing of the president, he was elected the official head of the local state party.

Over the next few years Pessoa tightened his control over the politics and political appointments of the state, thanks in part to his relationship not just with President Hermes but with his successor Venceslau Brás too, who took over in 1914. He also showed a ruthless side to his politics. For example, the former governor João Machado had expected Pessoa's fellow senator and ally Pedro da Cunha Pedrosa to stand aside in his favour. At the time Pessoa was just about to sail to Europe for what had become his customary holiday with his family. Surrounded by friends and politicians on board before he left, he announced in the presence of Machado that Pedrosa would not in fact be standing down. A furious

Machado had angry words with the new party boss before storming off. Later Pessoa accused him of *an act of indiscipline* and said he could no longer back him because he could *not support an enemy*. At the same time Pessoa also displayed some of the vanity and self-importance which critics were often to observe in him. He strongly denied that Hermes had assisted his return to power in his state. Instead, he insisted that his *return to political life* was the result of a *spontaneous and insistent offer from my people* to which the *President of the Republic didn't contribute in any way*.[3] Meanwhile at the national level, Pessoa was finally able to conclude some unfinished business in the Senate. Brazil's long-awaited Civil Code, which he had helped to kick-start when he was Justice Minister, was finally close to fruition. In 1915 the senator helped negotiate a compromise in the legislation that allowed it to be voted through at the end of the year.

One of the most striking examples of unrest that typified this period in Brazilian history came from the followers of an extraordinary Catholic priest called Padre Cícero Romão Batista in the north-eastern state of Ceará. Padre Cícero, who was said to have performed a miracle and seen a vision of Christ, became a hero to the many poor and dispossessed people of north-east Brazil and established a considerable following. At the same time he also became involved in politics and during the presidency

I cannot support an enemy.
EPITÁCIO PESSOA

of Hermes a group of his armed followers helped topple the governor of his home state when they arrived *en masse* at the gates of the town of Fortelaza. Their threatening presence alone was seemingly enough to force a change of government locally.[4] Even though it was only supported by the poor of the region, Padre Cícero's intervention was, albeit crude, still part of Brazil's political process, and the powerful and increasingly influential Padre Cícero struck deals with local political forces. Yet elsewhere Brazil saw a different form of dissent that became known as the Contestado and which, like the one at Canudos before it, was of a very different kind; one that represented a protest against the very system itself.

One of the key components of political power and government at a local level in Brazil during the First Republic was a phenomenon known as *coronelismo*. This refers to the process in which local strongmen – *coronéis* or colonels – controlled areas by dispensing favours and privileges in return for political support. Very often the *coroneis* were acting on behalf of their own masters, factions of the elites, meaning the colonels looked upwards in the power structure of society as well as downwards. They were the political middlemen, the power brokers, at work both in the cities and especially the countryside. Their power and precise role varied enormously, depending on where they were, the strength of local state machinery and their own personalities. Some were powerful enough to run what were in effect private armies in their own small fiefdoms. On occasion a colonel might be seen as a champion of the poor fighting against the rich and powerful – not unlike some of the celebrated bandits of the period who were feted as latter day Robin Hoods. One such rural leader seems to have been behind the creation of the Contestado movement.

The Contestado derived its name from the fact that it took place in an area whose ownership was still contested between the two southern states of Santa Catarina – which hired Pessoa as their lawyer and subsequently won the legal battle over the dispute – and Paraná. Its early leader was a man known only as José Maria, who was a healer and who was backed by one of the local rural bosses. José Maria, who some said was an army deserter, was credited with miraculous powers, and was even reputed to have raised someone from the dead. Around this colourful character gathered a cluster of followers drawn from the local countryside and villages, people who had lost their land and livelihoods thanks to the coming of the railways, timber companies and expropriation, and railway workers who were no longer needed by the companies. By 1912 the authorities sensed this movement was a growing threat to social order and sent a small contingent of troops to quell it. As in the earlier rebellion of Canudos, the authorities completely underestimated the strength and ferocity of this part-religious part-social protest movement and the troops were fought off. José Maria himself was killed, though his martyrdom seemed only to inspire his followers, many of whom expected their leader to rise from the dead. Meanwhile, and more prosaically, the rebels demanded land. It was not until 1915 that a contingent of 6,000 troops was able to quell the Contestado movement and even then elements of the protest lingered on until 1917. It was a reminder that there was more than one Brazil; and that many of the country's poorest members felt they had little or no stake in the society the nation's leaders were constructing.

POPULAR PROTESTS
The First Republic was punctuated by social unrest, in addition to the political strife and threat of military revolts. In the countryside these were sometimes led by messianic leaders, who offered the poor and dispossessed social justice and were often linked with conservative pro-monarchy, pro-Church sentiment. In the coffee plantations there were disputes and clashes, and in 1913 a limited series of strikes at Ribeirão Preto in São Paulo state. Urban protests in the First Republic were mainly confined to the period 1917–20. In addition there were groups of bandits or *cangaceiros* who lived outside the law and were often seen as heroic figures by the poor.

The different examples of Padre Cícero and the Contestado movement show the importance of religion in such popular movements. This was manifested in other ways too. In the Amazon jungle there were periodic religious awakenings among the indigenous Indian peoples. These were a hybrid of Catholicism and traditional religions and superstitions – which often had an impact on beliefs in rural Brazil – and were often explicitly opposed to what they saw as the misery imposed by the civilisation of the white man. Yet another example of the importance of religion came a little earlier at the end of the 19th century in southern Brazil. A woman called Jacobina Maurer claimed she was the reincarnation of Jesus Christ. One of the interesting points about her was not just that she was a woman – but that her movement took place among Brazil's German immigrant population.

German settlers had been arriving in significant numbers since the third decade of the 19th century, largely in the south of the country and especially in the states of Rio Grande do Sul, Santa Catarina and Paraná. Initially encouraged by Dom Pedro I, the immigrants – some of whom had a military background – continued to arrive for several decades. There was a slowdown in the middle of the century thanks to an 1859 German ban on sponsored emigration to Brazil. This followed complaints that colonists had been ill-treated. But by the start of the 20th century there were at least 200,000 people of German extraction in southern Brazil, with some claiming the true figure was up to half a million. In Santa Catarina and Rio Grande do Sul the German settlers tended to live in relatively isolated villages and, while some integrated well with local Brazilians and other nationalities, many settlements preserved features of their German heritage – including their language. There were, for example, a number of

German-language newspapers such as the *Deutsche Post* and the *Deutsche Zeitung* in Porto Alegre.

The presence of the Germans in Brazil became an issue on the eve of the First World War, as tensions mounted in Europe. The overwhelming majority of these immigrants had gone there, as had so many others, simply for the chance of a better life in the New World. Yet the concentration of Germans in a sparsely-populated land captured the imagination of a few German thinkers with rather more grandiose ideas. For example, in 1911 a German writer in Europe spoke contemptuously of the 'dismal picture of South American civilisation' and said he hoped the 'immense plains of La Plata … will fall into the hands of the German people'. He claimed it was 'truly a miracle that the German people did not long ago resolve on seizing the country'. Such lurid claims could be dismissed easily, but it was harder to ignore the views of one of Germany's best-known economic historians of the time, Professor Gustav von Schmoller. Writing in 1910, he stated: 'We must desire that at any cost a German country containing some twenty or thirty million Germans may grow up in the coming century in South Brazil … no matter whether it remains a portion of Brazil or becomes an independent empire or enters into close relationship with our empire.' However the official – and sincere – German government position was that they had no designs on territory in Brazil.[5]

Relations between the German Brazilians and their compatriots were complicated. It was not unusual for Brazilians of German extraction to rise to the highest levels in society. An example was Lauro Muller, who became Foreign Minister after the death of Rio Branco in 1912. Yet many Brazilians of Portuguese extraction expressed surprise at the way Brazilian Germans often kept their distance and did not appear to make an effort to learn the Portuguese language and embrace their culture. In turn, a number of Germans in Brazil considered their host country's government and institutions to be corrupt and/or inefficient, felt many Brazilians were both arrogant and lazy, and considered the Portuguese language to be unimportant in world culture compared with German, English or French. In other words, stereotypical views of each other were quite common.

The outbreak of the long-expected war in Europe in 1914 naturally made such relations more complex. For the great majority of Brazilians of all backgrounds, the European conflict seemed a long way away and appeared unlikely to have much direct impact on their daily lives. Yet this did not mean they were all indifferent. The upper echelons of society mostly sympathised with the Allies, and especially with the French and Belgians. Brazilian education was based on the French system and many of the country's intelligentsia identified closely with French culture and history. The French Revolution, the Franco-Prussian War of 1870 and the Paris Commune were all key events etched in the minds of educated Brazilians. So even though Brazil had quickly declared itself neutral in the conflict, moral support lay largely with the Allies. Immigrants of Italian descent – Italy had been an ally of Germany but kept out of the war until it joined the Allies in May 1915 – and German settlers naturally felt differently. A few Germans even volunteered for action and were killed fighting for their country on the battlefields of Europe. More typical, however, was a fund-raising campaign to collect money to help the German Red Cross and orphans and war widows.

Not all of the non-German Brazilians were sympathetic to the Allied cause either. Those army officers who had trained in Germany before the war wrote newspaper articles to counter what they saw as anti-German propaganda, even if they generally hid behind pseudonyms to do so. In the south those Portuguese-Brazilians who recognised the work-ethic of the German immigrants sprang to their defence, calling for an end to verbal attacks on all things German. One national figure, Dunshee de Abranches, President of the Chamber of Deputies in the National Congress, championed the Central Powers' cause, praising the success of the German Empire and dismissing the war as being more about commerce than anything else. For such views he was regarded as a hero by the local German-language press.

More typical, however, was the way the majority of the Portuguese-language press in Brazil portrayed events in Europe, in particular running reports of alleged German atrocities. The German-language press meanwhile had their own take on events, and eventually hit back at what they considered the pro-Allied anti-German bias. Dr Wilhelm Rotermund, publisher of *Deutsche Post* and a senior clerical figure in the German community, used the columns of his own paper to attack what he called the lies being written about the Central Powers. He also felt the Germans had little to apologise for in wanting to preserve their culture. 'We have gone much too far in our politeness,' he argued. 'Why don't the [Portuguese-Brazilians] learn German?' These remarks were picked up by the Portuguese-language newspapers and inevitably caused bitter controversy. In the ensuing row the *Deutsche Post*'s offices were lucky to escape being burnt down.[6] Yet despite the fact feelings were running high and most Brazilians supported the Allied cause, there was as yet little or no sign that Brazil had any appetite to get directly involved in what still seemed, from South America, an exclusively European war.

Soon, however, Brazil was to find that even the breadth of the Atlantic Ocean could not stop the effects of the war reaching it.

4
Brazil at War: 1917–18

Though the shocking accounts of the muddy trenches of the Western Front seemed remote from Brazil, it was not long before the grim conflict started to make itself felt there too. Even before war had started, the economy had shown signs of stalling. In particular, problems had hit the volatile rubber industry whose brief boom had led to the development of the remarkable Amazonian city of Manaus, which boasted an opera house and which was the first large Brazilian city to have street lighting. The problem was competition from cultivated rubber tree plantations in Asia, which were far more efficient and productive than the industry in Brazil, where owners tapped wild trees. (Attempts to cultivate Brazil's own rubber trees largely failed.) The astonishing growth of rubber production in the East took most people, and especially the Brazilians, by surprise. In 1900 the Asian plantations exported just 4 tonnes, a figure that had soared to 107,000 tonnes by 1915. By 1922 the East would be responsible for more than 90 per cent of all international sales of this vital product. Brazilian rubber barons simply could not cope with the drop in prices and soon the opera house in Manaus fell silent, the docks were left idle and the warehouses began to moulder gently in the humid Amazonian air.

Coffee prices had also fallen just before the war and in 1913 the country suffered its first trade deficit since the end of the monarchy. With war now underway, this was the worst possible time for the country's economy to experience problems. In 1914 imports had fallen to half of what they had been a year before, and as Brazil's treasury relied heavily on import duties for its revenue, this was another major blow. Government spending slowed down, merchants faced losses or even went bankrupt and foreign banks quietly removed their gold from the country. One of the problems was that Europe – and especially London – was the financial centre of the world, where Brazilians and others went to raise loans to pay off debts or finance business ventures. Now the international credit system collapsed, and Latin American nations such as Brazil were especially badly hit. On top of that, Brazil was dependent on the free flow of international shipping both to import and export goods. The inevitable disruption caused by the war only underlined Brazil's vulnerability.

It was a tough time to take over as president. The new man was Venceslau Brás who was elected head of state in 1914 when President Hermes' eventful period of office came to an end. At least the transition to power had been a smooth one. Brás, a former governor of Minas Gerais, had been vice-president under Hermes and was backed by both his home state and São Paulo. He also retained Lauro Muller as Foreign Minister, his ancestry – he was born in Brazil of German immigrant parents – as yet no cause for public concern. In any case, at the start of the war many in Brazil – as elsewhere – assumed the conflict would soon be over. Moreover, when it became clear the war would continue for some time Brás, who was a patient politician, if an uninspiring one, was able to use the war to distract people from economic and social problems at home. The world crisis also provided an opportunity for the president to appeal for national unity. Indeed, one of the by-products of the war for Brazil would be an increase in identity and nationalism, and a gradual re-evaluation of its European roots in favour of its distinctive American heritage.

The war nonetheless raised specific problems for Brazil, in addition to the initial economic setbacks. Though President Hermes had been quick to signal Brazil's neutrality and its ports were closed to armed vessels from any of the belligerent nations, declaring neutrality and being able to maintain it were two different matters. To begin with, the country felt torn between competing loyalties. Brazil's ruling classes had deep cultural and historical ties with France and Britain, and close economic links as well, yet the country felt pulled in the other direction, too, and not just because of the presence of so many immigrants of German origin. The Brazilian army had been seduced by the efficiency of the German military machine. Economic ties were also growing, and by the outbreak of the conflict Hamburg had become second only to New York as a market for Brazilian coffee. Indeed, the presence of around two million bags of São Paulo coffee in German ports at the outbreak of war was, as shall be seen, to become a key issue for the Brazilian government when the war finally ended.

Brazil's neutrality was not, however, just under strain because of its split loyalties. There was also the question of whether the Brazilian navy would be able to maintain the neutrality of its own territorial waters. The already modest nature of its fleet was further undermined just before the start of the conflict when the British Navy took over three ships being built for the Brazilians on the Clyde in Scotland when the government was unable to pay for them. The *Javary*, *Solimoes* and *Madeira*, which had been destined for use as patrol boats on Brazil's rivers, were re-named the *Mersey*, *Humber* and S*evern* and put to work by the Royal Navy off the coast of Belgium instead. By 1917 Brazil's navy consisted of two modern dreadnoughts, two ageing coast-defence battleships, four cruisers, ten destroyers, four torpedo boats and an assortment of patrol vessels and submarines. Though not negligible, this was hardly a huge fleet for a country with an enormous Atlantic coastline and one that was utterly reliant on international trade.

The position on land was scarcely more encouraging. US observers in Rio regarded the Brazilian army as markedly inferior to its counterparts in Chile and Argentina, for all that its officers had been influenced by the German military. In addition, its troops were tied up for the early years of the war with internal disturbances, notably the Contestado rebellion. On the face of it there seemed little imminent threat of an invasion, even if the possibility of armed conflict with Argentina was always something that concerned the Brazilian military. Argentina, like the rest of Latin America, had also declared its neutrality in the war. However, there was the nagging doubt that Germany just might intervene militarily in a country where so many German immigrants lived. Though it may sound far-fetched today, this fear existed, and not just in Brazilian minds. In 1918 the Uruguayan president Feliciano Viera publicly stated that his government 'harboured very serious suspicions that the German government was fomenting an insurrection of German settlers with the object of promoting an uprising in the provinces of South Brazil'.

In the United States, President Woodrow Wilson's influential personal adviser Colonel Edward House was preaching the virtues of closer co-operation between the nations of the Americas, in part because of concerns over German designs on South America. In particular, House thought Brazil was the 'main object of Germany's desires'.[1] In reality the Brazilians had little or nothing to fear from the German armed forces nor indeed from the immigrants of German extraction, the vast majority of whom stayed loyal to Brazil, despite their sympathies for kith and kin.

A clear sign of the way in which many Brazilians from the upper echelons supported the Allied cause was the creation of the League for the Allies (*Liga pelos Alliados*) in the spring of 1915, which attracted a number of important figures. Among these was Rui Barbosa, the celebrated 'Eagle of the Hague', orator and statesman. Another was Pessoa's old classmate from law school José Graça Aranha, the novelist and diplomat. Aranha's novel *Canaan*, published more than a decade earlier, had painted an unflattering picture of the German community in Brazil, suggesting its members were mean-spirited. Meanwhile Barbosa raised questions over the role of Germany in the Contestado rebellion, amid claims that a German company buying up territory in the disputed area was selling land only to German settlers. The aims of the League were to defend the Allies in the press, raise money for the British and French Red Cross and promote the adoption of the Portuguese language among immigrants in the country. It also condemned what it saw as German atrocities in the war. Another aim was to counter some of the pro-German propaganda and the actions of part of the German community. Small sections of the community had done themselves few favours by setting off fireworks to celebrate German battlefield victories, singing 'Deutschland über Alles' and flying German and Austrian flags. Later in the war the growing sense of patriotism was manifested in the creation of organisations such as the League of National Defence, established in September 1916. This body's stated aim was to protect the country from attack from both outside and within and it became increasingly influential as the war dragged on. It urged Brazilians to join rifle clubs that had been set up around the country, encouraged the Boy Scout movement and was a public platform for promoting moral education and the importance of civic duty.

Amid the gloom of the reports from Europe's battlefields and the tensions at home, Brazil did at least show some signs of recovery after the dark days of 1914. Though coffee was hardly an essential commodity and its export was hampered by increased shipping costs, the industry fared reasonably well, and even experienced a mini-surge in exports to Germany as that country temporarily found a way around the Allied blockade. Exports to the United States increased too, reaching around a half of all Brazil's sales. Rubber fared less well, even though the industry maintained its level of production and briefly benefited from a rise in prices in 1916. Other less high-profile industries such as cocoa in Bahia and sugar in Pernambuco (which benefited from a temporary rise in prices during the war) manganese and livestock products in the south, also helped the country recover from the worst of its economic woes.

Though Brazil was far from isolated in world trade during the war, the growing demands of the Allies and in particular countries such as Britain created anger and resentment. At the heart of this resentment was what was called Britain's Black List. From as early as 1915 Britain realised that economics and trade were additional weapons in the Allied war against the Central Powers. In 1916 Britain passed the Trading with the Enemy Act which, as its name suggests, was intended to stop British firms or subjects from having any trade relations with enemy citizens or companies. The British government drew up a list of such enemy outfits known as the Black List. The Americans suspected the Black List was essentially a policy of economic imperialism in Latin America designed to bolster the country's long term trade prospects. It certainly caused considerable offence in Brazil, where British consular officials reportedly tried to enforce it with some zeal. For example, coal was essential to the boats that plied their trade on the huge river system in the southern states of Brazil. But those steamboat operators that had German connections were refused British-sourced coal.

In August 1916 the Brazilian Foreign Ministry formally protested to the British representative in Rio, Sir Arthur Peel, about the actions of British officials. It cited an example where British officials had threatened to blacklist a company formed by Brazilian and Portuguese businessmen merely on the grounds that it was being marketed by a Brazilian and Portuguese firm that had a handful of German shareholders. The response of the British authorities was not entirely sympathetic, simply promising to investigate the matter while reiterating the reasons why the Black List was deemed necessary. Though the list did not provoke any permanent diplomatic breaks, it was a real irritant for the authorities and the wider public at large. Gradually the realisation that Brazil's economic well-being was being compromised by what were seen as the Allies' uncompromising and selfish tactics helped engender a sense of economic nationalism during and after the war. Nor was Britain more popular when in 1917 she banned the importation of coffee. The British already had enough coffee and wanted to free up vessels for more essential wartime supplies.

Though overall Brazilian sympathies undoubtedly lay with the Allies, there was still no clear sign at the start of 1916 that it might reconsider its neutrality. This policy was not reviewed even when news of Brazil's first casualty of the war was announced in May 1916: the sinking of a Brazilian steamer by a German submarine. The ship was called the *Rio Branco*, the name of Brazil's late and much respected foreign minister. Inevitably the initial reaction in the Portuguese-language press was one of outrage. 'To combat this infamous Prussianism is the duty of all nations,' proclaimed one newspaper.[2] The Brazilian foreign minister Lauro Muller immediately demanded an explanation from the German authorities, who were quick to reaffirm their friendship towards Brazil. It soon turned out the ship, despite its name, had been leased by a British company and was flying under British colours at the time of the incident, and moreover no Brazilian lives had been lost. The issue swiftly went away.

Soon afterwards, however, the mood against Germany started to harden. It was sparked by the veteran statesman Rui Barbosa during a typically eloquent and provocative speech shortly after the sinking of the *Rio Branco*. The occasion was Argentina's celebration of 100 years of complete independence from Spain in July 1816. Anxious not to be accused of insufficiently respecting its neighbour's latest national celebrations, Brazil sent a delegation to Buenos Aires headed by the celebrated Barbosa, who was warmly greeted by his hosts. Before an audience of distinguished diplomats and ambassadors he gave a powerful speech in which, as at the Hague, he emphasised the rights of small nations and the responsibilities in international law of countries at a time of war – including neutrals. 'No nation can be a law unto itself,' he declared. 'None can be an indifferent spectator in this world tragedy.' Neutrality entailed obligations, he insisted, before adding: 'Between those who destroy the law and those who uphold it, neutrality is not permissible. Neutrality does not mean impassibility; it means impartiality, and there can be no impartiality between right and justice on the one hand and crime on the other.'[3]

The speech had a considerable impact, and not just on the immediate audience. It was widely perceived not just as an attack on alleged German atrocities but also representing growing unease within Brazil over its neutral status. It was also seen by some as criticism of Woodrow Wilson's studied support of US and Latin American neutrality at this time and his perceived failure to speak up against the actions of Germany. The inescapable logic of Barbosa's speech seemed to be that Brazil should join the war on the Allied side. Certainly many assumed he was representing official Brazilian thinking. This view was enhanced when both houses of Congress voted to publish the speech as part of their official proceedings. Yet the Brazilian government quickly disassociated itself from Barbosa's comments. In general Venceslau Brás and his foreign minister Lauro Muller, who himself harboured presidential ambitions, gave a good impression of not quite knowing how to react to events in Europe. It was admittedly an awkward situation for Brazil, caught between its American obligations and its pro-European sentiment. Though they were far from slavish in following the American lead, practical diplomacy demanded that ministers took account of their northern neighbour's policy. And all the while the US stayed firmly neutral, Brazil had to stay neutral too – to do otherwise would expose herself to attack from German ships and submarines without the proper means to defend herself. Nor indeed, despite the acclaimed words of Rui and increasing press vitriol aimed at the Germans, was there any real sign the Brazilian public itself was clamouring for war.

Nonetheless, relations with Germany began to deteriorate further during the course of 1916. The entry of Portugal into the war on the Allied side – following on from Italy the previous year – inevitably had an impact on public sentiment in a country with many immigrants of Italian and, of course, Portuguese origin. The failure of the German authorities to offer what the Brazilians regarded as acceptable terms of compensation for the coffee that had been trapped in Hamburg had already caused considerable anger. In addition, there was frustration at the lack of merchant shipping available to help export and import goods, a problem caused by the conflict. One potential solution was to requisition formally the more than 40 German vessels that had been languishing in Brazilian ports since the start of the conflict. One deputy in Congress even drew up a bill to carry this out. But Brás and Muller were nervous this might be construed as an act of war, and the measure was dropped.

The mood began to tip decisively towards ending neutrality early in 1917. In January of that year Germany announced it would attempt to impose a full blockade around Britain and other Allies. This move provoked the US to break diplomatic relations with Germany on 3 February 1917, but it also sent shockwaves through Brazil. For a country that depended on the seas and on Europe for its trade, such a blockade was bound to have a serious impact. In a communiqué on 9 February the government in Rio spoke of the 'imminent menace of the unjust sacrifice of lives, destruction of property and the complete disturbance of commercial transaction'. It therefore announced that 'in spite of its sincere and anxious desire to avoid disagreements with the friendly nations now at war' it had no option but to make a formal protest. It noted ominously that responsibility for 'all events' that happened to Brazilian citizens, ships or goods as a result of the blockade would lie firmly with the Imperial German government.[4]

It was now clear to Brazil that Germany and the US would soon be at war, and that this would have a knock-on effect on Brazil's position. Muller was still reluctant to follow the US's lead and break off diplomatic relations with Germany, however, to the evident disappointment of Washington. Instead, the Brazilian foreign ministry engaged in private talks with other Latin American nations, apparently aimed at holding a peace conference to discuss the worsening crisis. It seemed that the Brazilian government was flailing around, trying to work out what to do next – a state of affairs that reflected both Muller's declining influence and President Brás's natural tendency towards inaction.

The event that changed the mood in Brazil and propelled it towards war came on 5 April 1917 when news reached Rio de Janeiro that a Brazilian steamer, the *Paraná*, had been sunk by a German submarine 12 miles off the French coast. What made this dramatic news even worse were reports that five shells were fired at the ship just before she went down, and that the German submariners made no attempt to rescue the crew. Three of the crew members died; the rest were saved by two passing French warships and a British merchant vessel. Brazilian public opinion was outraged, and tempers were hardly calmed when the German authorities initially claimed the ship had been sunk by a French or British mine. In Rio crowds gathered in the Avenida Rio Branco and sang the 'Marseillaise', the French national anthem, while others attacked German-owned property. There were similar demonstrations and disturbances in São Paulo, as protestors chanted pro-Brazilian and anti-German slogans. The mood was heightened by the fact that the US had just declared itself at war with Germany. But the worst of the unrest came in Porto Alegre in the south where there was a sizeable German population. In three days of rioting, some 300 buildings with German connections were destroyed or damaged, including the well-known Hotel Schmidt which was attacked by arsonists. In parts of the German quarter householders took to flying the Brazilian flag to dissuade protestors from attacking them.

Even with such a strong mood sweeping the country, the government in general and the foreign minister in particular prevaricated. Lauro Muller apparently still hoped that a simple warning to Germany might be enough to enable Brazil to continue its neutral policy. But eventually he was overruled by tougher voices in the government, and on 11 April the country finally broke off diplomatic relations with the Kaiser's regime and took into 'protective custody' – effectively confiscating – the 43 German merchant ships in its ports. Yet even then the government sent out mixed messages, as it allowed the German representative in Brazil, Adolf von Pauli, to take his time in departing. And on 25 April Brazil announced that it still maintained a neutral position between the US and Germany – meaning that American warships would be unable to use Brazilian ports.

Many foreign observers looked on with bemusement and frustration at Brazil's reaction. Some criticism was aimed at the indecisiveness of President Brás, but most was directed towards Lauro Muller. One US diplomat, Alexander Benson, who believed the Foreign Ministry was in a state of 'utter demoralisation', was especially hostile, describing the Foreign Minister as 'selfish, shifty and utterly unscrupulous'.[5] At the same time a number of senior figures in Brazil now called for Muller to be sacked and replaced with Rui Barbosa. Barbosa himself openly criticised diplomatic timidity in a typically forthright speech in Rio. Perhaps inevitably, Muller was suspected of having pro-German views and of delaying the government's response to what was seen as German aggression. In fact, though he had undeniably been cautious in his approach during the war, there is no reason to suppose Muller had any particular pro-German bias in his policy, though he doubtless had a greater understanding of the German point of view than many. His undoubted desire to keep Brazil neutral stemmed from his conviction that this was the right policy for Brazil rather than from support for the land of his parents.

Muller was a mainstream politician with good connections – his cousin Felippe Schmidt was governor of Santa Catarina – who had played a role in the election of Hermes da Fonseca. As foreign minister he had essentially followed the cautious pro-US policy established under his illustrious predecessor, at the same time being credited with improving relations with Argentina and Chile – the other two members of the so-called ABC group of nations in the Southern Cone area of South America. Yet as the war dragged on and anti-German sentiment grew, Muller's origins became more of a factor, as he himself was aware. A story that circulated told how at a reception held in his honour, the host's young son had asked what Muller was – apparently meaning what his profession was. Misinterpreting the question Muller innocently responded, 'I am a German'. Muller himself always denied that his ancestry affected his approach to politics, claiming that the only time he felt German was 'when I see a bottle of beer'. On another occasion he angrily declared: 'I am a Brazilian and only a Brazilian!'[6]

Despite his protestations of patriotism and his counter-attacks against the 'demagoguery' of men such as Rui Barbosa, it was now clear Muller's days were numbered. A press campaign – which amounted to a smear campaign – was in full cry, amid allegations he made contemptuous and derogatory remarks against Brazilians in private, and that he was now a hindrance to President Brás. On 3 May 1917 Muller resigned as Foreign Minister and was replaced by Nilo Peçanha, who had briefly taken over as caretaker president when President Afonso Pena died in 1909. The move signalled a clear shift towards a more assertively pro-American and anti-German policy.

Events now began to move more swiftly. Later in May the Brazilian government learnt that another ship, the *Tijuca,* had been sunk off Brest and on 1 June Brazil formally ended its neutral status in relation to the US-German conflict, following yet another speech in the Senate by Barbosa. Soon afterwards part of the US fleet arrived in Brazilian waters, a reassuring sign for a country that now feared her maritime trade would be targeted directly by German submarines. Later that same month Brazil revoked her neutrality in relation to the war between Germany and the Allies. At the same time the 43 German ships in Brazilian ports were formally commandeered. The fate of these ships dominated Brazil's diplomacy for several months over the southern hemisphere's winter and into its spring. Both Brazil and the Allies in Europe wanted to make use of the ships, but there was considerable wrangling before the French finally leased 30 of the vessels.

Meanwhile, behind the scenes, some apparently sinister

information had come to light about Germany's intentions in South America, and especially Brazil. The German minister in Argentina, Count Karl von Luxburg, was a colourful character noted for his use of robust language in his despatches. At the time many of these were routed to Berlin via Swedish diplomatic channels and were written in code. Copies of some of the despatches were leaked to the US ambassador in Buenos Aires, and eventually through co-operation with British Intelligence in London – which had cracked the Swedish code – the messages were deciphered. Some of them proved to be explosive. In one dated 7 July 1917 von Luxburg had written to Berlin: 'Our attitude towards Brazil has created the impression that our easy-going nature can be counted on. This is dangerous in South America where the people under a thin veneer are Indians. A submarine with full power to act might save the situation.' A month later another despatch stated: 'I am convinced that we shall be able to carry through our principal political aims in South America, the maintenance of an open market in Argentina and the reorganization of South Brazil, equally well with or without Argentina.'[7] These appeared to support the fear that Germany really did have plans to intervene in Brazil. The country had been rife with rumours about such plots, one of the more absurd being that Felippe Schmidt had at his command an army ready to take on Brazil's own military. No such force existed of course, and General Schmidt himself was part of the Brazilian military. The telegrams, however, seemed to show that there was some substance behind the rumours.

The Americans did not go public with this material, instead handing the contents through diplomatic channels to Buenos Aires and Rio de Janeiro. Brás and the new Foreign Minister Peçanha decided to continue their waiting game and chose not to use the messages as a pretext for declaring war on Germany – as the US had doubtless hoped they would. Instead they calculated that the von Luxburg despatches were a useful card to be played at a later date. In October it emerged that the Germans had torpedoed yet another Brazilian ship, the *Macao*, this time off the coast of Spain. To make matters even worse, the Germans had taken the ship's commander captive. A few days later on 26 October 1917 the Brazilian Congress voted overwhelmingly for a resolution declaring Brazil and the Central Powers to be at war. This made Brazil the only South American country to go to war with the Central Powers, though seven Caribbean and Central American republics including Cuba, Honduras and Panama did so.

Brazil's first act of belligerence was to try to seize the German gunboat *Eber* in port in Bahia, though the crew thwarted the attempt by scuttling the vessel. It was now, too, that Peçanha chose to make use of the von Luxburg telegrams, announcing publicly that details of a German plan to invade Brazil had been exposed. This rather overstated the contents of the telegrams, though few people at the time bothered with such detail when the texts of the decoded messages were published in newspapers. Meanwhile President Woodrow Wilson sent effusive congratulations to his Brazilian counterpart. 'Your action [in declaring war] in this moment of crisis tightens the bonds of friendship which have always held the two republics together,' said the US commander-in-chief.

In Brazil itself the news of war was greeted with more anti-German rioting and government restrictions on the German community in Brazil. In this so-called *Lei da Guerra*, on 16 November 1917 restrictions were imposed on businesses and banks with German connections. In addition

German-language newspapers were ordered by the government to stop publication, and only those schools that taught in Portuguese were allowed to stay open, while a number of German sailors were interned. Meanwhile, the inhabitants of some German-dominated towns in Santa Catarina telegraphed the president pledging their loyalty to Brazil.[8]

Yet though Brazil had finally joined the war, it was far from clear what, if any, practical impact the country could have on its outcome. Unlike the US, there was no question of Brazil's army being capable of sending thousands of troops to the battlefields of Europe. Brazil's navy was in slightly better shape, but it was again uncertain what role it should play. Indeed, before Brazil had joined the war a frank and confidential assessment by a British official was that the South American country could best assist the Allied cause by being 'friendly' rather than by joining in the conflict itself. Nonetheless Nilo Peçanha declared Brazil was keen to do its duty and by the end of the year plans were put forward to increase Brazil's army from 24,000 men to 54,000. Senior military figures were also despatched to the United States and Europe to discuss the re-equipping of the Brazilian forces and to find out what role its troops and ships *could* play. A military mission under General Napoleon Aché was also sent to liase with the French military close to the fighting on the European mainland. Some of its officers even took part in action and were cited for bravery. There was also talk, though little more, of sending Brazilian troops to fight alongside the British in Mesopotamia. The Brazilian representative in London, Fontoura Xavier, argued that his countrymen would be better suited to that country's climate than the British.

The chief role of the Brazilian navy, meanwhile, was to help patrol the South Atlantic, an area thought to be vulnerable to the establishment of German submarine bases. Then in December 1917 the British government invited Brazil to send a small squadron to work under the British Admiralty. Brazil enthusiastically agreed and two cruisers and four destroyers were overhauled and finally set sail from Rio on 14 May 1918. The squadron's first mission was off the west coast of Africa, where its task was to clear German mines and keep the waters open for Allied merchant shipping. In the autumn the Brazilian fleet received fresh orders and set sail for the Mediterranean. However by the time it arrived at Gibraltar, the main British naval base in the area, the war had already ended.

A less likely form of potential Brazilian involvement was in the air. Brazilian interest in aviation went back to the exploits of Alberto Santos Dumont, who was born in Brazil but had moved to France where he had become a celebrated aviator before the war. Interest in aviation grew even stronger after what turned out to be an embarrassing misunderstanding involving the British monarch. On 27 November 1917 King George V hosted a meeting in London with Fontoura Xavier. The meeting was a chance for the diplomat to hand over a communication from President Brás regarding the South American country's entry into the war. Unfortunately King George appears to have gone beyond his brief by suggesting that Brazilian airmen might be able to come to Britain to be trained to fight for the Allies. Even more unfortunately, Xavier told the foreign ministry back in Rio, who immediately informed the press. For a while the Brazilian newspapers were full of talk about the King's 'offer'. The reality was rather different. The British already had more pilots than aircraft, and were in no position to host extra pilots from Brazil. The British minister in Rio, Sir Arthur Peel, was ordered to make this point to Nilo Peçanha. The Foreign Minister, however, understandably pointed out that this left Brazil in a difficult situation. The news had already been made public, a number of airmen had volunteered and the public now expected their aviators to go and fight in Europe. In the end a compromise was reached and it was agreed that just ten Brazilian airmen should go to Britain. Other aviators were sent to Italy, while the Brazilian authorities also did a deal with the Italians and French to import a number of aircraft. It seems possible that had the war lasted another year, Brazilian airmen could have played an active role.

A rather more tangible way in which Brazil contributed to the war effort was through medical assistance. The population had already raised money for the Red Cross in Europe. Now that she was part of the war, Brazil's own Red Cross took a more active role and sent a team of 100 surgeons under Dr Nabuco de Gouvêa to France in mid-1918. A number of the doctors took their wives, who worked as nurses alongside them. This medical mission worked in various field hospitals and also set up a hospital in Paris with 300 beds. After the war this was donated to the University of Paris. It was a role that was acknowledged and appreciated by the French authorities and public.

Brazil's biggest help to the Allied cause, however, was probably economic, by exporting foodstuffs to help keep Europeans fed during the conflict. In 1914 for example Brazil exported just one tonne of chilled beef. By 1916 this figure had leapt to 33,600 tonnes and by 1917 the total amount was more than 66,000 tonnes. Less dramatic but still significant rises in exports during the war related to beans and sugar, the latter industry enjoying a brief revival in fortune. Another product of importance was manganese, which was used in munitions manufacture. Deprived of Russia's supplies because of war and revolution, and with supplies from India going to fulfil Britain's needs, the US was able to turn to Brazil for this crucial commodity.

The importance of Brazil to the Allied war effort should not be overstated. Its military input was minimal and one can say with certainty that it had no bearing on the outcome. Some commentators at the time were dismissive of Brazil's efforts, notably on the German side. One historian suggested that Brazil 'only theoretically took part in the war'. An American observer in Brazil meanwhile noted that the war failed to rouse real passion among the people, with public opinion showing 'almost complete apathy' by the spring of 1918. The same commentator said Brazilians of German origin were scornful of the war effort. '[They] look with derision upon the "play-war" which this country is indulging in,' he wrote. For good measure he claimed that the application of the war laws aimed at the German community was a 'hollow pretence'. It was certainly true that the enforcement of some wartime rules varied from state to state and in a number of respects were quietly ignored. The Brazilian federal authorities also had a relaxed approach to their laws on German firms and banks, realising that enforcing them too strictly hurt Brazilian society as a whole as much as the German companies. According to one study, too, a large number of small businessman of German origins suffered little loss: '...most had to endure nothing worse than patriotic suspicion, innuendo, or an occasional harsh word or insult.'[9]

Yet Brazilian assistance in the war *was* appreciated by its allies, as shown by the warmth of a letter from the British minister in Rio, Sir Arthur Peel, to the Foreign Minister Nilo Peçanha in the autumn of 1918. Sir Arthur rightly pointed out that Brazil had joined the war effort at a time when the outcome was 'most uncertain' and indeed when Allied victory appeared 'more distant than ever'. After outlining Brazil's practical contributions to the war, the diplomat noted the 'hearty cooperation of the Brazilian people who have never failed to manifest their sincere and whole-hearted sympathy with the great cause for which we are all fighting, a moral support of inestimable benefit.' All these various forms of support and goodwill 'cannot but be warmly appreciated by nations engaged in a death struggle for the cause of liberty and the triumph of justice'.[10]

The war had other repercussions for Brazil too. Just two decades earlier she had refused to send delegates to the first Hague Peace Conference on the grounds that it could have no relevance. Now the country had taken an active if limited part in this most bloody of European wars and was fully engaged in diplomatic activity both within the Americas and with European powers. Indeed one consequence of the war was that – for a time – it reversed a tendency that had been moving in the opposite direction and drew it closer once more to its European allies. At the same time another phenomenon had begun to grow more powerful, that of Brazilian nationalism. These contradictory forces would jostle with each other over the coming years as Brazil came to understand the reality – and limitations – of its impact abroad. First, however, there was barely disguised excitement at the thought of Brazil taking a seat at the forthcoming Conference that was to take place in Paris to sort out the various peace treaties required to bring a permanent end to the conflict. It was a golden opportunity for a Brazilian delegation to rub shoulders with the most powerful nations in the world and demonstrate its new-found authority as a Latin American power. All that remained was to decide who would be in the delegation.

One candidate for a place on the team was likely to be Epitácio Pessoa. He had enjoyed what could be called a quiet war, at least when it came to national politics. Much of his time and effort from 1915 to late 1918 appear to have been absorbed by events in his native Paraíba. He was the state's senator and his and his allies' grip on local affairs was to last for another decade and a half. These were what were sometimes called the era of the 'order of Epitácio Pessoa'[11] in Paraíba, which contrasted sharply with the chaos of the previous years. This did not mean, however, that Pessoa himself was often in his home state. Instead he preferred to stay with his wife Mary and their three daughters at their home in Rio de Janeiro, where federal power lay and where he felt he could have more influence.

This hands-off approach to state politics did not endear him to everyone. The author Osvaldo Trigueiro, whose family had close links with Pessoa's family, noted that politicians in the distant northern state felt unable to discuss problems and complaints with the region's leading political figure. Communications between Rio and Cabedelo in Paraíba were tough at that time, the train journey taking from six to eight days. According to Trigueiro, this was a journey that Pessoa preferred not to make himself, and even if the local politicians decided to make the journey to Rio to meet with him, it seems the aloof lawyer did not go out of his way to be hospitable.

'As a leader, [Epitácio] knew how to keep his distance, and wouldn't permit intimacy,' wrote Trigueiro. 'On Mondays, he would receive Paraíbanos in his home in Rua dos Voluntarios da Patria [in Rio] – although he never went to the station to pick up or take any of them. I can't remember any lunch or dinner with any of our senators – in the same way, he would rarely invite them to his house.' In fact, the Brazilian author believed that Pessoa could not be considered a skilful politician simply because of his offhand manner, unwillingness to compromise and an ingrained old-style oligarchic view of life and politics. 'He didn't have the capacity to convince, the desire to be conciliatory, or the gift of popularity,' Trigueiro continued. 'Aristocratic of manners, and with a feudal mentality, he was the opposite of an able and clever politician. He was proud of facing crises and keeping friendships.'[12]

On the surface, Pessoa himself seems to have agreed with at least part of this somewhat blunt assessment. In April 1917 he wrote to the state's governor Camilo de Holanda that because of his ill-health – he complained of problems with his nervous system – and because of what he termed the *incompatibility* between his personality and the political demands placed on him, he wanted to quit as state party boss. However, the letter may simply have been part of his political manoeuvring, for Pessoa showed no outward signs of wanting to relax his tight grip on state politics, despite his clear preference for life in Rio. And although Pessoa publicly advocated *free and honest* elections in his state and urged respect of the law – as he had done all his adult life – this did not stop some of his followers resorting to intimidation and even violence to ensure the right result in local elections.[13]

Though he was immersed in local politics and privately complaining of illness, Epitácio Pessoa was now on the eve of the four most important years of his life. A noted international lawyer, shrewd negotiator and former government minister, and with an intimate knowledge of Europe, Pessoa had the ability, experience and status to be a natural contender for Brazil's delegation to Paris. Soon, however, events would conspire to propel the man from Paraíba even further into the political limelight.

Pessoa driving to Mansion House in London, 14 June 1919.

II
The Paris Peace Conference

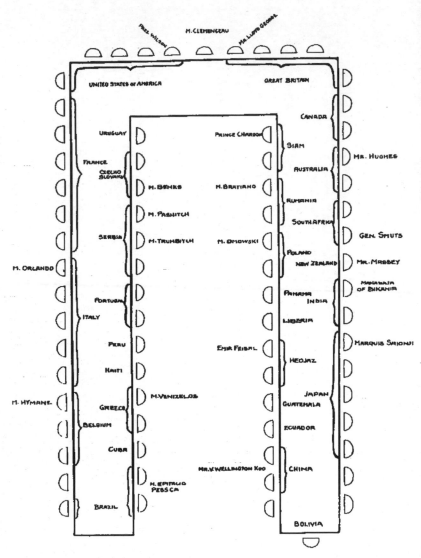

Sketch of the seating plan at the Paris Peace Conference.

5

Paris 1919

Despite relief and joy at the Allied victory and the relative strength of the economy, these were uncertain political times in Brazil. The influenza pandemic that swept the world at the end of the war hit Brazil at around the time of the armistice in November 1918. At the same time Venceslau Brás's difficult, though by no means disastrous, presidency had come to an end. His successor was Rodrigues Alves, who had already been president and who was regarded as a popular choice by most factions on the Brazilian political scene. Unfortunately, however, he was in poor health and though his new cabinet was announced on 15 November the President himself was too ill to take up his duties.

The President's incapacity contributed to the confusion and ultimately embarrassment that surrounded choosing who would lead Brazil's delegation to the Paris Peace Conference. The obvious candidate for this prestigious post was the ageing Rui Barbosa. He had the advantage of being well-known and admired in Europe and elsewhere in the world, not just for his eloquence at the Hague conference in 1907 but also for his speeches in support of the Allied cause during the war, most particularly his famous speech in Argentina. Accordingly Barbosa was formally invited to head the delegation, an invitation that was repeated by Rodrigues Alves despite his illness. It seemed like a done deal.

Unfortunately, there were other factors at play. One was the pride of Rui Barbosa, a man who could be as stubborn as he was loquacious. The other was behind-the-scenes manoeuvring by opponents of the appointment. A key figure in the controversy was Domício da Gama, who had spent seven successful years as Brazil's ambassador to Washington. Now da Gama was the new Foreign Minster, a position from which he could direct Brazilian diplomacy during the negotiations in Paris. It seems clear that da Gama was worried that Barbosa was such a powerful and forceful character that he would both upstage the Foreign Minister and prove impossible to control. There are even suggestions that da Gama may have coveted the position of delegation leader himself. In a 'private and confidential' telegram to the Foreign Minister on 24 November 1918, the Brazilian Embassy in Washington noted: 'Your Excellency's travel to Paris seems timely. Your influence with the Americans will play a key role in Congress and your personal contact with the main heads of state of the other countries will increase Brazil's prestige and facilitate greatly the solution of any Brazilian issues.' Whatever his precise aims, da Gama's opposition provoked a controversy in the Brazilian press about who should head the delegation. Many newspapers pressed Barbosa's case, as da Gama acknowledged in a message to the Washington embassy on 26 November. Inevitably, Barbosa's pride was wounded and he felt his position was being undermined. He was also hurt by the fact that some of the other members of the delegation had reportedly been appointed without his knowledge.[1]

Torn between his strong desire to go to Paris and his hurt pride, Barbosa ultimately decided to turn down the invitation. In a tone of anger and sorrow Rui wrote to the ailing President: 'There is no greater sacrifice to which I could subject myself than to refrain from executing your urgent wish, the wish of the legislative bodies and of the nation in general, by not going where my heart would lead me, where many times I have hoped to go – to Versailles, to finish what I began at The Hague and what I continued in Buenos Aires.'[2] Da Gama had got his way.

If Barbosa had been an obvious choice, his replacement was less so. But it was now that Epitácio Pessoa's decision to stay in Rio at the heart of national politics reaped its reward in an unforeseen way. Already touted as a member of the team, he was now invited to head the delegation. Though he certainly lacked the stature of Barbosa, he was nonetheless a shrewd choice. His greatest weakness was that he lacked direct diplomatic experience. His greatest strengths included the fact that he was a lawyer, with experience of international disputes from his work on boundary issues under Rio Branco. He also understood the inner workings of the First Republic, and had maintained close contacts with many people at the top of Brazilian politics. In addition he was a regular visitor to Europe and knew the culture well. Yet, although well-disposed towards European society, he was not seen as being antagonistic to the United States. This could not always be said about Rui Barbosa.[3]

For a brief period at the end of the war, Brazil had been courted by both Europeans and the US. In particular, Britain and France had ground to make up after the dislocation in international shipping caused by the war and in London's case by the friction caused by the controversial Black List and ban on coffee imports. Italy, too, sent officials to Brazil during 1918 in order to build up economic links. France's position was strengthened by the fact that Brazil chose French officers to take part in a military mission to the Brazilian army to help with training.

On the other hand, the United States held a strong position in relation to Brazilian trade, having boosted exports to the South American country during the war as well as having imported products such as coffee and manganese. However, Brazil and US trade relations had not always gone smoothly during the war either. On one occasion Brazil briefly suspended exports of manganese to its northern ally following a brief spat over American coal supplies to Brazil. One problem was that Brazil often felt – not an uncommon feeling among Latin American countries – that the United States never paid it the attention or respect it deserved. It was certainly true that elements in Washington took the relationship with Brazil for granted. Brazil was also deeply frustrated that the US happily continued its trade and strong links with Argentina, which had resolutely stayed neutral in the war to the bitter end. For the Brazilians this showed a lack of understanding. After all, it was they, not the Argentineans, who had gone to war on the US's side.

This was the complex diplomatic backdrop against which the shrewd but diplomatically inexperienced Epitácio Pessoa was to be pitched as leader of the country's delegation at Paris. The make up and size of the rest of the delegation was to prove no simple matter either. True to his rather autocratic manner, Pessoa insisted he should have full say over who should make up the other three members of the four-man delegation, plus the experts and support staff who would accompany it. One of these was João Pandiá Calógeras, an experienced politician from Minas Gerais who had been both Minister of Agriculture and Trade, and Minister of Finance. Another was Olinto de Magalhães, a medical doctor but more importantly Brazil's man in France. There was, however, a dispute over who should be the fourth full delegate. By coincidence a Brazilian state deputy, Raul Fernandes, was having to travel to Europe at the time with his wife, who needed medical treatment. To help fund his trip Fernandez volunteered his services to the President as one of the delegation's secretaries. The ailing Rodrigues Alves agreed to his request, but was unhappy that a state deputy should work as a mere secretary, so insisted he be a full delegate instead. Pessoa was unhappy at having Fernandez imposed on him and instead suggested he become his legal adviser – a position the deputy turned down. Much to Pessoa's annoyance the President overruled him and Fernandez was made a full delegate, with the international law professor Rodrigo Octávio Menezes fulfilling the role as legal adviser. According to one observer, Osvaldo Trigueiro, Pessoa remained unhappy with the decision for some time. 'Raul Fernandes told me that Epitácio never forgot the episode and at first didn't forgive him. During the voyage from Rio to Portugal, their relations were distant and formal,' he said.[4]

Even this was not the end of the matter, as the scale of the Brazilian delegation came under threat from another source – international horse-trading between the so-called Great Powers: the US, Britain and France. The question for these victorious Allies was not just who should be invited to attend the Paris Peace Conference in January 1919 but also what their status should be. The US State Department was keen for Latin American nations to take part, but only those who had joined in the conflict. This was good news for Brazil, as it boosted its standing in relation to its neighbours, notably Argentina and Chile. Rio was also pleased at Wilson's unexpected decision to lead the US delegation himself – even if the decision was greeted with less than delight by the French and British. After all, it could hardly harm Brazil's prestige to be seen negotiating side by side with the President of the United States of America – even if President Wilson had rather tarnished his image in many Latin American eyes after his country's recent military interventions in Mexico. However, Brazilian pride at the prospect of being Latin America's favoured nation at the conference was dented when reports emerged in late November 1918 of a new development. The Great Powers had agreed that before the Peace Conference proper there would be what was billed an Inter-Allied conference first. Brazil was invited to attend as a member of the victorious Allied side but only as a 'belligerent power with a special interest' and not as a 'belligerent great power'.[5] This meant it would be permitted at best two, and possibly only one, formal representative.

This was a bitter blow for Brazil and especially for Foreign Minister da Gama. He claimed to have close links with the United States, and yet now seemed unable to guarantee his country's special status at the conference table. Da Gama hastily contacted the State Department to express his alarm. An official called Frank Polk relayed a message to Secretary of State Robert Lansing, who was already in Paris for the Conference. Polk said it was important to avoid humiliating da Gama and by extension Brazil. This would only bring comfort to Brazil's rivals Chile and Argentina who, as he pointed out, had not joined the war effort. He added: 'Brazil has stood loyally by us in practically every question that has come up in South America.'[6]

Lansing and his boss President Wilson were sympathetic to

Brazil's predicament, even though they had already agreed to the new conference arrangements. The Europeans were less so. The harsh reality was that for France and Britain the issues at stake in Paris far outweighed the question of how many coffee beans they imported from Rio de Janeiro. For France the preoccupation – obsession almost – was what to do about Germany, its belligerent neighbour. Britain meanwhile was primarily concerned with the balance of power in Europe and the maintenance of its empire. Relations with Brazil, though not wholly unimportant, were well down the list of priorities for British Prime Minister David Lloyd George and French Premier Georges Clemenceau, even though the latter had visited the South American country before the war. Wilson, too, had more pressing matters on his mind – not least his proposal for a global organisation that could help ensure the world never experienced such a conflict again. Yet he also advocated a new way of doing things on the world stage, of encouraging fresh openness between nations. And Wilson was genuinely keen that Latin America play a bigger role in the world, even if this was to be on his rather than their terms.

The plea by da Gama bore fruit. To convince his sceptical allies, Wilson pointed out that Brazil had a population of more than 30 million, a fact he said earned it the right to special treatment. He also pleaded the case of the Americas in general, saying it needed to be well-represented at the Conference. More speculatively – but perhaps preying on French fears – the American President also pointed to Brazil's large German population, even suggesting that in the space of another generation the country might become 'wholly Germanised'. The main opposition to Wilson's championing of Brazil came from Lloyd George, who suspected the United States was simply trying to boost the number of delegates

PRESIDENT WILSON'S FOURTEEN POINTS, 8 JANUARY 1918

The program of the world's peace, therefore, is our program; and that program, the only possible program, as we see it, is this:

I. Open covenants of peace, openly arrived at, after which there shall be no private international understandings of any kind but diplomacy shall proceed always frankly and in the public view.

II. Absolute freedom of navigation upon the seas, outside territorial waters, alike in peace and in war, except as the seas may be closed in whole or in part by international action for the enforcement of international covenants.

III. The removal, so far as possible, of all economic barriers and the establishment of an equality of trade conditions among all the nations consenting to the peace and associating themselves for its maintenance.

IV. Adequate guarantees given and taken that national armaments will be reduced to the lowest point consistent with domestic safety.

V. A free, open-minded, and absolutely impartial adjustment of all colonial claims, based upon a strict observance of the principle that in determining all such questions of sovereignty the interests of the populations concerned must have equal weight with the equitable claims of the government whose title is to be determined.

VI. The evacuation of all Russian territory and such a settlement of all questions affecting Russia as will secure the best and freest cooperation of the other nations of the world in obtaining for her an unhampered and unembarrassed opportunity for the independent determination of her own political development and national policy and assure her of a sincere welcome into the society of free nations under institutions of her own choosing; and, more than a welcome, assistance also of every kind that she may need and may herself desire. The treatment accorded Russia by her sister nations in the months to come will be the acid test of their good will, of their comprehension of her needs as distinguished from their own interests, and of their intelligent and unselfish sympathy.

VII. Belgium, the whole world will agree, must be evacuated and restored, without any attempt to limit the sovereignty which she enjoys in common with all other free nations. No other single act will serve as this will serve to restore confidence among the nations in the laws which they have themselves set and determined for the government of their relations with one another. Without this healing act the whole structure and validity of international law is forever impaired.

VIII. All French territory should be freed and the invaded portions restored, and the wrong done to France by Prussia in 1871 in the matter of Alsace-Lorraine, which has unsettled the peace of the world for nearly fifty years, should be righted, in order that peace may once more be made secure in the interest of all.

IX. A readjustment of the frontiers of Italy should be effected along clearly recognizable lines of nationality.

X. The peoples of Austria-Hungary, whose place among the nations we wish to see safeguarded and assured, should be accorded the freest opportunity to autonomous development.

XI. Rumania, Serbia, and Montenegro should be evacuated; occupied territories restored; Serbia accorded free and secure access to the sea; and the relations of the several Balkan states to one another determined by friendly counsel along historically established lines of allegiance and nationality; and international guarantees of the political and economic independence and territorial integrity of the several Balkan states should be entered into.

XII. The Turkish portion of the present Ottoman Empire should be assured a secure sovereignty, but the other nationalities which are now under Turkish rule should be assured an undoubted security of life and an absolutely unmolested opportunity of autonomous development, and the Dardanelles should be permanently opened as a free passage to the ships and commerce of all nations under international guarantees.

XIII. An independent Polish state should be erected which should include the territories inhabited by indisputably Polish populations, which should be assured a free and secure access to the sea, and whose political and economic independence and territorial integrity should be guaranteed by international covenant.

XIV. A general association of nations must be formed under specific covenants for the purpose of affording mutual guarantees of political independence and territorial integrity to great and small states alike.

sympathetic to its cause. In the end however the British prime minister skilfully used the issue to wrestle concessions himself, increasing the representation of countries from the British Empire.[7]

The outcome of this inelegant horse-trading was that Brazil's quota was raised to three rather than two delegates, a privilege also granted to Belgium and Serbia after they too protested. The news came as a relief to the Brazilian government and da Gama in particular. It was agreed that Brazil's planned fourth delegate, Olinto de Magalhães, would join the delegation anyway, though he would not be part of the country's formal negotiating team. Not every country was delighted with the outcome of this pre-Conference skirmish. Portugal had declared war on Germany before Brazil and had committed 60,000 troops, a far greater contribution to the war effort than anything the South American country had managed. Yet Lisbon was permitted just one delegate. In Rio de Janeiro, however, the fact that Brazil was allowed to have more delegates at this crucial conference than its old colonial master was hardly a cause for sadness.

ooooo

The Brazilian delegation, headed by Epitácio Pessoa, left Rio de Janeiro on 2 January 1919 bound for France. Symbolically, the delegation sailed on the *Curvelo*, one of the ships confiscated from the Germans during the war; the question of who owned those ships was to be one of Brazil's two key issues at the Conference. Pessoa was accompanied by his wife and daughter, Laurita, as well as the rest of the delegation and assorted secretaries, servants and members of the Brazilian press corps – many of them, too, with their families. This sizeable delegation took up just about all the berths on the ship.

It was a sedate trip, the *Curvelo* chugging along at a top speed of just 10 mph, to the growing frustration of Pessoa and the others. At least the slow voyage gave the delegation a chance to talk, with Raul Fernandez, the legal consultant Rodrigo Otávio and the expert naval consultant Armando Burlamaqui gathering in the smoking room to discuss strategy. However, soon the sluggishness of the *Curvelo* – not helped by some delays over refuelling – began to alarm Pessoa. The formal opening of the Conference was scheduled for 18 January, a date deliberately chosen by Clemenceau because it was the anniversary of Wilhelm I's proclamation as Kaiser of the new German Reich at Versailles in 1871. Now as their ship made its leisurely way across the Atlantic it was becoming increasingly clear to Pessoa and the rest of the Brazilian delegation that they were was going to be late for one of the most important international gatherings in recent world history. Despite his embarrassment, there was little he could do but alert the Foreign Ministry in Rio, and get them to warn Calógeras and Olinto de Magalhães, who were already in Paris, that the head of the delegation would be late, and to take appropriate action. On 15 January his telegram to Rio, headed 'Delegation of Brazil to Peace Congress – on board *Curvelo*' read: *Voyage much delayed. Maximum speed steamer 10 miles ... Believe will not arrive Paris before 27.... Maybe convenient Your Excellency telegraph Olinto in case debate comes to Brazilian questions can suggest delaying until our arrival seeing we bring documents proving our rights. Affectionate Greetings. Epitácio Pessoa*[8]

The growing certainty that they would be late for the Peace Conference was not the only issue that dampened spirits on board the *Curvelo*. As they came into European waters, the ship docked at Lisbon where Pessoa and his delegation learnt the ailing President Rodrigues Alves had finally succumbed to his illness. Not only would Brazil's main delegation not be present at start of the Conference, they would not have a president either. Moreover the acting head of state, Vice-President Delfim Moreira, himself not in the best of health, was regarded as a political lightweight. It was not the most auspicious of beginnings to Brazil's grand European adventure.

At last, on 28 January, the weary party arrived at Le Havre in France after a journey that had lasted nearly four weeks. The delegation and its retinue caught the first available train to Paris, only to discover their misfortunes were not quite at an end. Arriving in the French capital, they were greeted by heavy snow but no official welcoming party. Moreover, because of the poor weather it proved impossible to find a taxi. Eventually Pessoa and his family and other members of the delegation were given a lift by Dr Nabuco de Gouvêa, the man heading Brazil's medical mission to France during the war. They eventually arrived at the Hotel Plaza in the chestnut-tree lined Avenue Montaigne to enjoy a modest supper and tea sweetened with saccharine – a consequence of wartime shortages and something of a shock for representatives of what was once one of the world's great sugar-producing nations. Still, there was at last something to cheer the delegation up – a hotel worker had thoughtfully put a Brazilian flag alongside the French flag over the entrance to Pessoa's suite. Finally someone had noticed that the head of the Brazilian delegation had arrived.

Pessoa was well used to Paris, and the city held many memories for him. Not all of them were good – his first wife had died in childbirth there many years ago. Yet he can never have before encountered a Paris quite like this. It was a city that bore the scars of war, of which the lack of sugar was just one small example. Bomb craters still punctuated parts of the centre while jobless and wounded war veterans propped up street corners. Frequent demonstrations reflected the deep unease and uncertainty that prevailed over much of Europe at the time, a mood shaped not just by the effects of war, but also by the Bolshevik Revolution in Russia, which had a magnetic pull on radical politics across the continent. Revolutionary talk was in the air, and not just in Geneva.

However, Pessoa had little time for reflection on the contrast between the glamorous Paris of his youth and the uncertain city he now experienced. There were first of all a number of practical matters to be sorted. Though he, his wife and daughter were comfortably settled in a suite at the Plaza, the rest of the delegation were scattered across other establishments in the city centre at a time when accommodation was in short supply. This would make communications and transport more difficult. Pessoa also had to find room to set up his own secretariat. But most of his first full day in France was spent catching up on the latest developments, holding meetings and trying to

BRAZIL'S IMAGE IN EUROPE
It was not uncommon in the middle of the 19th century for Europeans (and also North Americans) to confuse Portuguese-speaking Brazilians with their Spanish-American neighbours. Though knowledge of the differences had improved by 1919, largely through trade contacts, the country was still dismissed by many Europeans as hot, full of disease, uncultured and dirty. The fact that Brazil had a large black former slave population also lowered its stature in many European eyes. The international prestige of erudite statesmen such as Rui Barbosa had helped alter the stereotypical image, while Foreign Minister Rio Branco made a conscious effort to improve the country's image by sending prominent – white – writers abroad on diplomatic missions.

ensure that no more valuable time was lost after his delayed arrival.

His first chance to experience the mood of one of the so-called Great Powers at the Conference came a few days later when on 1 February he met Clemenceau. It was a friendly meeting and gave the Brazilian a chance to gauge relations between the French premier and other major leaders. Later he telegraphed the Foreign Ministry in Rio to give his impressions after his first encounter with one of the Conference's dominant figures:

Cordial Reception. I reminded him of the affinity between Brazil and France and he responded adding the same ideas and declaring himself ready to help us defend our interests. He asked with insistence my view of the League of Nations, of which commission I am part, expressing himself in terms revealing a large divergence with [President] Wilson ...[9]

The knowledge that the League of Nations was providing a source of disagreement between its champion President Wilson and the French, who saw it as a sideshow to the main focus on Germany, underlined to Pessoa how delicate Brazil's situation was. On the one hand Brazil enjoyed good relations with France and was keen to maintain them. One of the crucial issues for Brazil was the fate of the German ships it had seized – and having leased 30 of them, France was now in a strong position to influence the outcome of any negotiations. However, at the same time it was the US who had bolstered Brazil's position at the Conference and who could prove a powerful ally in the forthcoming negotiations.

The astute Pessoa was clearly aware of the problems involved in this difficult balancing act. He had, indeed, already been informed by Calógeras that the French were 'hostile' to the Brazilians' claims. Nonetheless he said he was *encouraged* that Brazil would be able to reach agreements on their issues, though it was already clear that he thought the Americans would be more useful than the French or British. For this reason he suggested Rio show the US State Department and Lansing the text of Brazil's memoranda on the coffee and ships, so they could better understand what was at stake. However, the head of the Brazilian delegation was under no illusion that the key issues at the Conference were not being carved up between the Great Powers, despite all the talk of new diplomacy on the US side.

The shrewd Magalhães had already told Rio that Britain's main aim was to maintain the supremacy of its navy and extend its colonies at the expense of German ones, and that Britain and France saw eye to eye on most issues. He also glumly quoted a well-informed article in the French newspaper *Le Temps* on the eve of the Conference that noted: 'Equality doesn't mean all governments have to be consulted about all issues as certain problems don't interest certain states.' And now Pessoa himself informed the Ministry in Rio: *Here all will be decided exclusively [between] five great powers according to their interests or individual points of view while the presence of small nations is destined only to give the appearance [of a] liberal organization [to the] Conference.*[10]

> **Here all will be decided exclusively [between] five great powers according to their interests or individual points of view while the presence of small nations is destined only to give the appearance [of a] liberal organization.**
> **EPITÁCIO PESSOA**

Though Pessoa had quickly grasped the *realpolitik* of the conference and the limited role Brazil could play, his ability to steer his country's diplomatic course was hampered by practical concerns. He was still hard at work translating the delegation's memos into English so the British and Americans could understand them, having finished the French versions while he was at sea. His aim was to meet with key delegates before the negotiations started, and before the official presentation of Brazil's documents, in an effort to influence their views. But for that, he needed documents they could readily understand. There were other problems too that needed to be resolved. One was the cost of living in post-war Paris, where the shortage of goods had pushed up prices to the obvious surprise and dismay of the Brazilian delegation. *[Y]ou have no idea at all of the difficulty of life here. Housing, food, clothing, transport, all at fantastic prices*, complained Pessoa in a telegram message to Rio.[11]

The worst problem was the lack of transport for the members of the delegation. The Brazilians had tried but failed to hire a car, because of the costs involved. Taxis, even unofficial street taxis, were simply unavailable. In any case, Epitácio objected to using taxis on a permanent basis because he feared this would create a bad impression. *This embarrassment is harming the interests of the mission*, he noted, pointing out that he had had to scrap some meetings altogether because of the problems in getting around the city. Epitácio also rather pointedly highlighted the personal sacrifices he was making through the winter for the sake of his country: *Some times so as not to sacrifice the country's business or skip the duties of politeness I have had to walk long distances on foot through half snow half mud. I judge it indispensable the acquisition of means of transport. Just today Calógeras missed lunch with the Romanian prime minister through not having found transport; I could only arrive on foot.* He also made sure the Foreign Ministry understood that Brazil was worse placed than other countries when it came to transport. *Various delegations brought vehicles; the Americans alone brought 70 automobiles*, he said. He then suggested he could take matters into his own hands and buy a car himself. *I have been offered a luxury Renault in perfect state for thirty three thousand francs. To get out of this embarrassing and humiliating position in which I find myself as soon as possible I will buy this one which maybe I can re-sell at the end of the mission, with a small loss.*

Other problems included the scarcity and cost of accommodation, which was hitting married staff on fixed salaries especially hard, as well as those members of the team who had to be on hand and staying in the expensive Plaza Hotel. To solve this and to save money Pessoa proposed the delegation should all stay in one, smaller hotel. Such messages make starkly plain the importance Epitácio attached to status and image – both his own and his country's.[12]

Despite these relatively minor but time-consuming problems, Pessoa and his team were finally able to consider the key issues that faced them. All participants had their own self-interested agendas, no matter how these might be dressed up as matters of great principle. In Brazil's case, these issues were divided into two categories. The first were essentially narrow Brazilian preoccupations that had little or only partial bearing on any other issue at the conference; these were compensation for the coffee that had been held in German ports during the war, and the ownership of the German ships confiscated in Brazil – a question that admittedly touched on wider matters of what to do about confiscated Central Power vessels. To these the Brazilians initially and rather naively added the issue of compensation for the war effort, though the American delegation rapidly made them aware that this demand was unlikely to be met – certainly not for a nation that played such little active part in the war and had suffered little or no damage.

The other issues were wider questions that touched on global or pan-regional matters. Clearly Brazil had little direct national interest – and certainly no say – in key questions such as how Germany should be punished for its aggression and whether French troops should be stationed right up to the banks of the Rhine. However, after Rui Barbosa's performance at The Hague in 1907, it did have a track record in international legal issues and dispute settling – which ensured its interest in Wilson's pet plan for a League of Nations. Wilson had proposed an organisation that would provide a forum for solving major disputes between nations. Though the shape and scope of this international organisation was very largely controlled by the US, Britain and France, Brazil was to play its own small part in determining the membership of its ruling council.

Brazil's ability to influence the outcome of any of these issues depended primarily on the wishes of the so-called Great Powers but also on the structures the Conference created. As so often in large events of this kind, true power lay not in the big cumbersome councils, but in the smaller tight-knit cliques and committees surrounding them. The body on which all representatives of attending nations sat

THE IDEA OF THE LEAGUE OF NATIONS
The concept of an international body or court that could resolve disputes between nations – and avoid war – had been around for much of the 19th century. The 1899 Hague Conference – which Brazil chose not to attend – even set up the Permanent Court of Arbitration, though it did not play a major role on the world stage. The idea of an 'association of nations' that evolved into the League, was championed by President Woodrow Wilson. Britain and especially France were generally less enthusiastic about the idea, certainly in the form envisaged by the American President.

was the Plenary Conference, but this met just eight times and had little real power. Far more important was the Supreme Council or Council of Ten which consisted of the leaders from the US, France, Britain, Italy and Japan. In March this council shrank still further in size to four and ultimately to just three – with Wilson, Lloyd George and Clemenceau effectively running the Conference.[13] So much, then, for Wilson's promise of a new form of diplomacy. In addition there were various commissions set up to examine particular issues such as aviation, war reparations, economics, labour legislation and the League of Nations. Of these bodies the last two, and especially the one considering the League of Nations, were easily the most productive and effective.

Faced with this illusion of high-minded structures and the reality of business-as-usual politics between the Great Powers, the smaller nations such as Brazil did what they could to have an influence. They were like the characters Rosencrantz and Guildenstern in *Hamlet*; occasionally they made an appearance but quickly exited stage left without having much impact on the main dramatic narrative. Pessoa was nonetheless keen for Brazil to punch above its diplomatic weight if possible. His main chance to do this was on the League of Nations Commission, on which he sat and where he was able to help record a modest but important victory over the Great Powers. This commission was dominated by the Great Powers, who had ten representatives, to just five from other nations – one each from Brazil, Belgium, China, Portugal and Serbia. These were designated as 'powers with limited interests'. However, these countries objected to the hegemony of the greater powers and eventually, after heated debate, it was agreed to add four more countries to the commission – Greece, Poland, Romania and Czechoslovakia. There was then a battle over the representation of the smaller nations on the council of the new League – with Pessoa among those delegates, including the Belgians, pushing to get at least four of these nations represented. Reporting back to his masters in Rio in a telegram, Pessoa wrote: *I fought [the Cecil proposal], proposing four [countries to be] chosen directly by interested States. Other delegates showed the same sentiment. Cecil withdrew the amendment, our proposal prevailing.*[14]

The concession was certainly a notable victory for Pessoa, who had been able to use his considerable experience as a lawyer and debater to good effect. In her biography of her father, Laurita Pessoa goes even further, suggesting he created a bloc of smaller nations to defend their interests against the Great Powers: '… He became a noted figure among the delegates of the smaller powers – a type of living link between them and the representatives of the powerful nations … He directed the movement in reaction to the authoritarianism of the great powers, who wanted to restrict the small nations' participation in the work of peace and above all in the incipient League of Nations.' However, one has to be cautious. Laurita Pessoa admits herself that while her father 'gathered the delegates of the small nations' to work together on a joint plan, he 'did not, unfortunately, reconcile all the contradictory interests'.

And other witnesses suggest Pessoa was not necessarily the prominent figure on the League of Nations commission that his or his daughter's words might suggest. Colonel House, who also sat on the commission, recalled '… the observations of … Pessoa, while impressive, were not very frequent'.[15] Also, while he had a degree of freedom in the way he chose to act, Pessoa was answerable to da Gama in a way a man of even greater stature such as Rui Barbosa may well not have been. And even if he did try to co-ordinate the lesser powers as both he and his daughter suggested, his main concern was always the advantage his actions could bring to his country.

Indeed, no sooner had victory over representation on the League's council been gained, than the lawyer urged the Foreign Ministry in Rio to make sure Brazil became one of the first four smaller powers on the executive. He urged da Gama to use his influence with US ambassador Edwin Morgan to get him to telegram President Wilson and Secretary of State Lansing pleading Brazil's case. *Your Excellency understands the prestige such designation would give us. Brazil, the only South American belligerent, has in its favour special claims.* This effort proved successful and when the Plenary Conference adopted the League Covenant on 28 April, Brazil was confirmed as one of those four countries, along with Greece, Belgium and Spain.[16]

Pessoa strove to help his country's cause at the Conference by cultivating a good working relationship with President Wilson. It was a sound decision, as the US leader turned out to be Brazil's greatest champion in Paris. The two men met during the working of the League of Nations commission on which they both sat and which met in the luxurious surroundings of the Hotel Crillon, where much of the American delegation was based. At their first meeting Pessoa assured the President the Brazilian delegation would be keen to support the US on issues of special interest to them and hoped the US could reciprocate on issues of concern to the South American country. Pessoa was also delighted that when Wilson departed for Washington shortly after the draft Covenant for the League was presented to the Plenary Conference, the American had said goodbye to him personally. On the whole the Americans found him easy to work with – certainly far easier than Rui Barbosa would have been. He sometimes needed careful handling, however. According to one US diplomat who knew him, his main weaknesses were 'vanity and arrogance' and he was seen by the same source as a 'safe' rather than brilliant leader of the delegation.[17]

The battles Pessoa and the rest of the delegation had to fight over the issue of coffee and ships showed why it was important to have such a powerful ally. The British and especially the French were less than sympathetic to Brazil's claims over issues that seemed to them entirely financial and utterly peripheral to the main focus of the Peace Conference. This jaundiced view of the Brazilian claims was not helped by the obvious fact that, unlike France, Britain and the US, Brazil had not lost hundreds of thousands of men – indeed it had lost scarcely anyone at all. This dismissive view of Brazil did not escape Pessoa, who well understood that his country's lack of serious participation in the conflict undermined their position.

His concern grew when he learnt to his dismay that the medical mission – the only visible sign of Brazil's involvement in the war on mainland Europe – was about to be wound down. At the time there were 312 wounded soldiers in the Brazilian medical mission's hospital, and the French were hoping it could take in more. Instead the Brazilian government was about to close it and ask French hospitals to take care of its patients. For the Brazilian delegation in Paris, the timing could hardly have been worse. A worried Pessoa telegraphed Rio, warning that Brazil's motives in Paris were already being widely questioned. *The hospital services are rehabilitating us in public opinion. If the government suspends this, the recriminations will become even more aggravated, contributing to the difficulties of the delegation.*[18]

The first of the issues that led many observers to believe

Brazil's motives at the Conference were more mercenary than idealistic was that of its 'missing' coffee money. This was also the more straightforward to resolve, though it still posed technical problems. The state of São Paulo was the owner of more than 1.835 million casks of coffee trapped in Bremen, Trieste, Hamburg and Antwerp in 1914. Though the Brazilian government had stopped Germany simply confiscating the precious cargoes, São Paulo had become nervous and ordered the coffee to be sold at once. The proceeds – 125 million German marks – were deposited in a German bank, and after further negotiation it was agreed that the money was to be handed over when a peace treaty was finally signed. Pessoa and his team had prepared a lengthy legal argument on the issue. Their demand was that the money held by the Bleischroeder Bank in Berlin should be repaid to São Paulo with 5 per cent annual interest added and, crucially, at the same exchange rate as when the money was first deposited. This was important because in early 1919 one German mark was valued at under three cents, but had been worth 24 cents when the monies were deposited.

The issue was formally presented to the Finance Commission, on which Brazil was not represented. To the horror of the Brazilian delegation, the Commission initially decided it had no authority over what it considered essentially a private affair between the state of São Paulo and a German bank. The subsequent protests by Brazil changed the Commission's mind – but it made the situation even worse by declaring that the coffee money should form part of the overall German war reparations, a complex and deeply controversial issue. This was disastrous news for Brazil, potentially delaying any repayment for many years. Pessoa, drawing on all his legal skills, submitted new documents insisting this was not an issue of reparation for war damage but a simple case of returning an identifiable bank deposit to its rightful owner. Once more the Commission yielded before his protest, but once again it provided yet another unsatisfactory decision for the Brazilians. The Commission ruled the German bank should repay the monies immediately, as a separate issue from reparations – but that this should be done at the current exchange rate.

Frustrated at the constant obstacles to achieving what he saw as justice for Brazil's coffee producers, Pessoa privately approached Norman Davis, a Treasury official on the American delegation and a key figure on the Finance Commission. During the course of two separate meetings Pessoa tried to persuade Davis of the strength of the Brazilian claim. It seemed to do the trick; a few days later the American contacted the head of the Brazilian delegation to inform him that the commission accepted his country's arguments and the money should be paid at the old exchange rates and with interest of 5 per cent. This became the basis of Article 263 of the Treaty of Versailles. It was a victory for the Brazilian delegation and a triumph for Pessoa's legal and negotiating skills, but it came at a cost. There was a feeling that the Brazilians had been haggling over what was, compared with other issues at stake, a relatively trivial affair and the issue almost certainly cost the country considerable goodwill.[19]

The obstacles faced by Brazil over its second and more complex claim certainly suggested that patience with the South American country's incessant financial concerns was wearing thin. This involved the confiscated German ships. Brazil's position was straightforward: it demanded to be allowed to keep all the ships with the proviso it pay a reasonable price for them, money that would be offset against war reparations. The Great Powers, and especially France and

Britain, had other ideas, however. Their policy was that all seized German ships that had not been formally requisitioned and regarded as spoils of war should be allotted to Allied powers according to the amount of shipping they had lost in the war. Under this policy Brazil would be permitted just 25,000 tonnes of shipping – compared to the 200,000 tonnes of German ships she had confiscated. To complicate matters further, the majority of those confiscated ships – 30 – had subsequently been leased to the French. As the country now in possession of much of the disputed shipping, France was to prove Brazil's toughest opponent over the issue and it was Louis Loucheur, Clemenceau's trusted financial adviser and chairman of the Finance Commission, who made clear the Allied objections to Brazil's claims.

The Brazilian shipping claim provoked considerable emotion on all sides. Lloyd George was uneasy that a country that had contributed so little to the war effort could profit so 'enormously' from the seized ships. And when Brazil's claims that France's leasing of the ships implicitly accepted the South American nation's true ownership were rejected by the French delegation, it prompted an unhappy Pessoa to comment that he had not expected such *unjust treatment from our noble friend and ally*. The Brazilian press, too, turned upon what they saw as the ingratitude of the French, pointing out that Brazil had willingly leased the ships to its ally at a time of need rather than making more money by selling or leasing them to the United States. Pessoa's main legal challenge was to prove the narrow but crucial point as to whether Brazil had confiscated the German ships – i.e. taken over ownership – at the time it had taken possession of them. If it could not prove this, then technically the ships were subject to the Great Powers' policy of being shared out among other nations. The lawyer's bargaining on the point was probably not helped by the fact he himself had grave doubts over the strength of Brazil's case. *Legally, our position is weak. The act of the Brazilian government was not requisition, as it was enacted in a time of peace, nor was it capture, as it was not judged by the Court of Seizure*, he confided to the Foreign Ministry in a telegram. The case was further weakened, he said, by the fact that the Brazilian authorities had previously and repeatedly stated they had not sought ownership of the vessels. Pessoa wisely realised the problem demanded a political solution rather than a legal one.[20]

Once again, it was to the United States that Brazil turned. The Americans had themselves been granted an exemption from the shipping allocation principle, allowing them to keep the German vessels they had seized during the war. It was an exception that Pessoa now exploited. To underline Brazil's firmness on the shipping matter, he wrote to Lloyd George warning that his country would refuse to sign the Treaty of Versailles if it did not recognise Brazil's claims to the ships. Meanwhile, in a letter to President Wilson, he urged that the United States understand his country's difficult position. Pessoa's view was that either Brazil should share the same exemption as the US or that all countries should be compensated for all the ships they had seized, as he outlined in a formal complaint to the Council of Four in late April 1919.

As Pessoa had expected, the US were inclined to support their ally in the Americas, especially given that they themselves had already argued and won the case for keeping their own ships. In a letter to the head of the Brazilian delegation Wilson wrote: 'It is needless to say that the United States would never do anything intentionally or conscientiously that could injure Brazil's interests.' Pessoa also found a staunch ally in Wilson's key aide Colonel House, who reassured him the US would do all it could on the shipping issue. *House [said to me] … that in this subject he considered himself the representative of Brazil*, was his recollection of their meeting.[21]

One of Pessoa's concerns was that as the solution to the shipping matter was essentially political rather than legal, it had to be found during the Conference. To leave it for later, when all bargaining power was gone, meant a happy outcome would be unlikely. In this, however, he was to prove mistaken. Wilson's lobbying on behalf of Brazil did shift the other Great Powers, who were not keen to spend more time and energy on what was for them a peripheral matter. Britain in particular was content to allow Brazil to claim full ownership rights to the ships. France, however, was still unhappy and the Conference was to end without a final agreement being reached. It would not be until May 1920 that France finally recognised Brazil's claims to the ships and another ten months after that – when the leases expired – that the 30 ships in French possession were finally returned to Brazilian ownership.

As Pessoa and his team carried out the tough negotiations and attended the endless round of meetings, they were at least comforted by the knowledge that their financial and transport problems had eased slightly. The head of the delegation carried through on his promise to buy a car, acquiring a Renault for 32,000 francs and spending a further 4,000 on a chauffeur, spare parts and insurance. His staff, too, found life a little easier, after the Foreign Minster agreed to boost their monthly pay to help them meet the Parisian cost of living – though, to avoid pay differential problems, Pessoa prudently recommended these be considered exceptional bonuses for special services rather than forming part of their regular salaries. He was also surprised – and relieved – when the Foreign

Ministry wired payment for his bill at the Hotel Plaza. In a message to them the lawyer admitted that his own pay barely covered the accommodation costs *but I did not feel the right to complain.* Indeed, though the Brazilian delegation was involved in some tricky talks – and was getting some criticism for what was seen as its mercenary approach to the conference – Pessoa seemed positively to be relishing his time in Paris. According to his daughter – and biographer – who was present, 'Those who accompanied him closely rarely saw him happier or better disposed than during the work of the conference. He seemed a man excited by a mission to his measure and his taste – happy with it and happy with life.'[22]

6
From Delegate to President: April– June 1919

Epitácio Pessoa's high spirits during the first few months of the Paris Conference may well have had something to do with the dawning realisation he was close to getting his hands on a position he had never deemed possible – that of President of Brazil. If his own words and reactions are to believed, he had previously given no thought to the possibility of becoming president, even after learning of Rodrigues Alves' death *en route* to Paris. This was not surprising. Though the Vice-President Delfim Moreira had made it clear he had no interest in the presidency himself, and that there would have to be a new election, the reality of Brazilian politics in the First Republic was that power was carved up between the big states of São Paulo, Minas Gerais and Rio Grande do Sul. Politicians from smaller states – for example those in the north-east such as Pessoa's home state of Paraíba – were effectively excluded from candidacy. Yet in early 1919 there was a problem in the usual triangular decision process. The governors of São Paolo and Minas Gerais were both relatively young men, and moreover Minas and Rio Grande ganged up to oppose a São Paulo candidate this time round. This made it impossible for the three states to agree on a suitable candidate. And then there was the question of what to do about Rui Barbosa.

Barbosa was one of the dominant personalities in Brazilian politics of his generation and one of the few who was known internationally. He was admired for his political courage, his intellect and the power of his oratory. Yet age had not quenched his fires, and he was a maverick, an independently-minded man who could be both disdainful and stubborn. Above all, should he ever be elected to the top job, he would most certainly not be the kind of malleable president the states' power brokers preferred. So when the former Foreign Minister Nilo Peçanha nominated him for the 1919 presidency, there was considerable scrabbling behind the scenes among the politicians of the three main states to agree on a candidate – any candidate – to keep Barbosa from office. This was what led to them choosing for the first and only time in the First Republic a candidate from outside the magic circle of states – Epitácio Pessoa from Paraíba.

Pessoa was formally nominated in early 1919 by the Minas Gerais politician Raul Soares. For Soares and the other oligarchs, he was an acceptable compromise. He was well connected in national politics, but had no particular allegiance to any one of the three big states. He was clearly a very intelligent and able man who had held high office, without ever having been a dominant figure nationally – and thus had no independent power base. He was also on an important mission for his country in Paris, and meeting regularly with the most powerful men in the world, ensuring that Brazil's new leader would have both a ready grasp of diplomacy and a network of personal relationships to call upon. Finally, there was little in his background and personality to suggest he would rock the political boat in Brazil and pursue a dangerously independent line.

But there were also more personal reasons why the choice of Pessoa was welcomed among the Brazilian elite. Back in 1917 when Rodrigues Alves had been proposed as a candidate for the presidency, the Paraíban had given a well-received speech of support in his position as senator. Later that same year he gave another speech in which he praised the personal qualities of the future president – a man who had already held the position before. Rodrigues Alves was a man *formed by moderation, order, respect for the law, intellectual patriotism*, one who had *reached the highest positions without aiming for them.* His return to the highest office in the Republic made him *able to be an example to the youngest, a lesson of leadership in a new country.*

> The possibility of my candidature [for the presidency] was not even envisaged when I left Rio de Janeiro for Paris.
> EPITÁCIO PESSOA

Some of Pessoa's supporters were later to wonder if there were not some prophetic element to the speech, with their leader cast as the younger generation who would learn the lessons of the old master. The speech was well received by Rodrigues Alves himself and the late president's family were subsequently happy to welcome Pessoa's candidacy – a significant factor in the Brazilian political system where family ties and connections counted for so much. However, most observers accepted he had not envisaged himself as president and that he did not actively seek the candidacy. In an interview with a French newspaper in Paris he insisted the news he had been chosen to be the presidential candidate *astonished* him. *I had carried out no lobbying on my behalf and my name was not put forward [by me], the possibility of my candidature was not even envisaged when I left Rio de Janeiro for Paris.*[1]

Indeed, when Pessoa first started to receive celebratory telegrams in February 1919 his cool reaction appears to have been genuine. The telegrams congratulated him without explaining for what, and he seems to have assumed that he was being praised for his conduct at the Peace Conference. When in late February his friend and fellow delegate Olinto de Magalhães telephoned to offer his personal congratulations to the presidential candidate, Pessoa simply laughed. *How is this possible, friend Olinto. Can't you see this is a joke?*[2] It was only when a telegram arrived on 25 February from the national republican convention in Brazil officially informing him of his candidacy he was certain the reports were accurate and he could be sure he had the highest office in his grasp. In theory he was of course no more than one candidate for the election. There was still the election to come and a formidable opponent to beat – Rui Barbosa. But the Paraíban politician knew he had the full backing of the most powerful clique in Brazilian politics. Even though the election campaign was taking place thousands of miles away from Paris, and without his active participation, the outcome was already a foregone conclusion. Epitácio Pessoa was all but certain to become the next president of Brazil.

The first question Pessoa had to consider after hearing the news of his candidacy was at which point he should return home. The poll was to take place in the middle of April and by now it was already the end of February. Even if he left for home immediately, this would leave him little time in Brazil before the election was held. Moreover, he was currently heavily embroiled in the Brazilian delegation's difficult negotiations on coffee and ships, as well as being involved in the process of setting up the League of Nations. It seems he gave little thought to returning home immediately; indeed, by early March he made it clear he would not even be heading back to Brazil straight after the election. Questioned by a French reporter on the subject he replied: *It will simply be the head of the state representing Brazil at the conference in place of a senator – that's all!*[3]

Back in Brazil itself, the old warhorse Rui Barbosa was preparing himself for one last political fight. His obstinacy, determination, loquacity and intellectualism had never been in doubt. To this the veteran now added another ingredient – anger, both with himself and others. Barbosa had quickly seen the folly of his decision not to head the Brazilian delegation to Paris. Having thrown away that chance of a last political hurrah, he had now seen his slim chances of the presidency disappear as erstwhile backers switched their allegiance to Pessoa. To lose out once to the Paraíban lawyer was bad enough; to be beaten by him again was insufferable. So despite his age and the hopelessness of his cause, Barbosa decided to fight one final battle, and set off on a gruelling tour of the country where he could speak directly to the electorate.

As Barbosa barnstormed around Brazil, his opponent was equally busy half a world away, sitting in meetings in elegant Parisian hotels and attending lunches with the great and good. Pessoa's own election programme – if it can be called such – was to promote the speech he had given 18 months before in praise of the late president. It may not have amounted to a detailed and coherent plan for government, but as both Pessoa and his powerful backers knew, it was more than enough to be certain of victory. The restricted number of voters and the way the electoral system was controlled by a complex system of patronage ensured this. However, he showed he was not entirely the yes man that some of his backers back in Brazil may have expected him to be. Well before voting took place, he stated publicly that the fact that someone from *one of the smallest states in Brazil* had been chosen as a candidate was a sign of a new direction in the internal politics of Brazil. *Up until now the big states alone had influenced matters and all our presidents in the Republic have come from among their ranks. I represent the first exception to this regrettable tradition that seemed to get out of hand: and this will be welcomed by all Brazilians with the same satisfaction which I myself feel.* [4] Such views, published far away in France, had no impact on the course of the election nor did they cause any visible misgivings among his powerful sponsors. But they were an early sign that Epitácio Pessoa might take a more independent line as president than many imagined.

The April election took place with little violence or unrest, a cause for some satisfaction. As expected, Pessoa was elected, winning 249,342 votes against Barbosa's 118,303, though the defeated candidate scored well among the emerging urban middle classes, winning a number of the major cities. At his Paris base congratulatory messages poured in, not just from Brazil but from the governments of other nations too. However, Pessoa was still in the thick of negotiations over Brazil's case to be on the League of Nations council and the rancorous debate over its confiscated German ships, another issue that would only be sorted out at the end of the month.

There is little hard evidence to suggest Pessoa's new status as president-elect increased his delegation's negotiating power. But it certainly boosted his personal prestige, and soon he was receiving invitations from governments across Europe and the rest of the world. Belgium, Italy, Britain, America, Spain, Portugal, Holland, Canada, Peru, Chile and

Argentina were all keen to play host to the soon-to-be head of the Brazilian state. Naturally he was unable to accept all the invitations, but he was keen to visit those nations with whom trading links would be important in the future – and with whom he regarded good relations as a priority. Thus his choice of countries to visit gives some clue as to the potential direction of his foreign policy. It was also becoming clear that Brazil was well on the way to meeting its own limited objectives at the Conference – getting compensated for the coffee and keeping ownership of the ships – while its place on the League of Nations council probably exceeded expectations. At this point in the Peace Conference the focus of the Great Powers was almost entirely on the issue of Germany and the exact terms of the treaty they were expecting it to sign. A country such as Brazil was merely a bystander to this central event – as Pessoa had known they would be from the start of the Conference. Therefore the President-Elect had more time on his hands and less urgent matters to deal with. It was now time to go travelling.

> Up until now the big states alone had influenced matters and all our presidents in the Republic have come from among their ranks. I represent the first exception to this regrettable tradition.
> **EPITÁCIO PESSOA**

Pessoa's first trip was in April 1919. He was invited by the French authorities to visit the Western Front where fighting had ended only the previous autumn. It was a chance for the Brazilian to get a personal glimpse of the true horrors of the war. He and his hosts left Paris for Soissons and then Reims before spending a day and night at Verdun – the scene of one of the most terrible battles of the war. The sights of the battlefield and of the local population understandably had a profound impact on Pessoa. In a speech at the Sorbonne soon afterwards, the President-Elect spoke of the *destroyed towns, ruined cathedrals, charred land and a population reduced to poverty, without homes or bread*. But he also took the opportunity to praise what he called the *spirit of resistance and vitality* and the *incomparable genius of the Latin race* by which he meant the French. Indeed this became a theme of Pessoa's as in a number of speeches he went out of his way to praise the achievements of the Latin peoples and in particular the French, despite or possibly because of his tough dealings with them over the German ships. It was also a way of under-lining Brazil's own Latin roots and the genuine affinity the Brazilian people – or at least its educated elites – felt for the French at this time.[5]

Back at the Peace Conference, events were approaching a dramatic climax. On 7 May the terms of the Treaty were finally handed over to the newly-arrived German delegation in a tense meeting at the Trianon Palace Hotel. Pessoa, though, had little time to dwell on this momentous occasion. The very next day he set off for Brussels, as guest of the Belgian monarch King Albert. The King had been grateful for Brazil's early condemnation of the German invasion in 1914 and this was a chance for the Belgian people to show their apprecia-tion. In contrast with his low-key arrival in France, Pessoa found himself greeted by the King and Queen in person at the railway station before being escorted to the royal palace. The Brazilian had last been to Belgium as a tourist in 1894 and he saw how the country had changed. Though he thought the country looked back to normal on the surface, he said he was horrified by the destruction of much of Belgium's industrial base at the hands of the Germans, and promised that Brazil would do all it could to help the country recover.

In what was otherwise a highly successful trip, there were two slight difficulties. One was that Pessoa was offered the Grand Cross of the Order of St Leopold – the highest honour the Belgian monarchy could bestow. According to his daughter, he had some qualms as a republican about accepting a royal honour, though in the end the prestige of his country – or just maybe personal vanity – won out and he chose to accept it. The second issue was money. By now he had set out a timetable for his return to Brazil, trying to dovetail this with the diplomatic visits he judged vital to his country's interests. After Belgium he was planning to visit Italy, Britain and Portugal before sailing to the United States and Canada and then home. However, as the President-Elect was finding, state visits do not come cheap. In Belgium alone he spent 16,500 francs, including gifts to help the charity work of the Queen, Mayor of Brussels and the Church, plus the cost of transport and feeding a total of ten people in his entourage. He also spent 3,000 francs on what he called *tips* for the palace staff. Now he was worried about the cost of his next visit. *Train trip to Italy more expensive. Believe will have to give alms there as well*. At least, he thought, he would be *excused such a contribution* in Britain and the US. But the likely costs still caused him to telegraph home to see if the Foreign Minister could help out. He also later asked for an extra £30 to help out with the expenses of the Brazilian ambassador to Belgium. Money for these trips was to be a constant issue with Pessoa.[6]

Despite the concerns over money, this was an exhilarating time for Pessoa. But it also emphasised just how peripheral the smaller nations – including Brazil – were to the main agenda of the Peace Conference, namely the German question. In May and June 1919 the leaders of the Great Powers at the Peace Conference were still agonising over the content of the treaty they expected Germany to sign. The Germans had been horrified at what they saw as the brutal and humiliating terms of the Treaty and there were powerful voices back home urging its delegation not to sign. On the Allied side Lloyd George was said to be having second thoughts about the terms of the Treaty, too, which he and some others in the British delegation felt was too harsh on Germany. Yet for Pessoa such weighty matters were not at the top of the agenda. Instead, as the lesser nations looked on powerless while the great drama unfolded, his main aim was to foster good relations with key potential allies before returning home to take up the presidency.

It was not all fun, either. The Brazilian's train trip to Italy was a gruelling one, lasting a full 30 hours. He was rewarded on his arrival on 19 May by being met by Vittorio Emmanuele III and Queen Elena. During his three-day visit he also had an audience with Pope Benedict XV. The Vatican had not been invited officially to the Peace Conference, partly because of what was seen by the Allies as the Pope's unhelpful call for peace during the war and especially his 1917 Peace Plan, which had been rejected by President Wilson. The Pope was also to pronounce himself unhappy with the outcome of the Paris Conference. Yet the meeting provided a chance for Pessoa to cement relations between the Vatican and Brazil whose people, as the statesman was at pains to point out, held the Pope in profound respect. Indeed, in despatches back to Brazil, the President-Elect considered himself well content with the reception he received in Italy.

Back once more in Paris, Pessoa had time to attend a lavish banquet at the Elysée Palace hosted by French President Raymond Poincaré and was also awarded the Légion d'honneur by the French authorities. However, he scarcely had a chance to assess the diplomatic situation in Paris before he was whisked off to London at the start of June as the guest of King George V. One added complication was that the work of League of Nations commission – in which the Brazilian delegate Calógeras was involved – was now being transferred to London. This meant that for a brief period Rodrigo Otávio was left in charge of the dwindling work of the Brazilian delegation in Paris as its two senior members left. In London Pessoa, once more accompanied by his wife and his daughter Laurita, was greeted by the Prince of Wales on behalf of King George V at Victoria Station. A delighted Pessoa was also met by members of the British government. But what struck him most was the friendliness of the cheering crowds he encountered in the London streets.

By now Pessoa knew he could not spend much more time in Europe. Already he was receiving telegrams from Brazil asking him, as he put it, *with greatest urgency* to return home to take up the presidency. It was not that Brazil was undergoing a crisis; but the acting president Delfim Moreira, who was in poor health, showed no inclination to carry on as head of state. This growing sense of urgency caused him to turn down a request to visit Madrid, as he had already done so for Switzerland, Chile, Peru and Cuba. He was genuinely sorry he could not visit Spain, a country for which he had *always had the most lively personal sympathy and with which Brazil maintains such valuable commercial relations.*[7] Yet to squeeze in a trip to Madrid would mean not just delaying his return to Brazil, but also his important journey to the United States, and he had agreed to be in New York by 19 June. Ahead of this the Brazilian still had to keep up a promised visit to Lisbon; given the historic relationship between the two countries it would have been difficult for him to have turned down this request. As it was, he had to make use of a British warship, HMS *Renown*, in order to get to Lisbon on time.

At last Pessoa was ready to cross the Atlantic once more, five months after he had made his way to Paris for the Conference. Yet in an unfortunate symmetry with his first trip, the Brazilian and his team were once more delayed. He had found it difficult to find enough space on a ship going to the US. His entourage included not just his wife and daughter but his secretarial team and servants too. An additional member was an American State Department official, Herbert Stabler, who had put himself at the Brazilian's disposal during the Conference – another sign of how the US and Brazil worked closely together in Paris – and whom Pessoa now insisted should travel with them to New York. Ultimately the President-Elect pulled a few strings with the French government and was able to travel on board the French warship *Jeanne d'Arc*. At first all was well, as the cruiser steamed towards the Azores. Then disaster struck.

Pessoa's telegram to the Brazilian legation in Washington from on board the *Jeanne d'Arc* on 16 June was marked VERY URGENT. It read: *Owing to break down in her engines* Jeanne D'Arc *is unable to proceed on voyage. STOP. Our situation may become dangerous from one moment to the next. STOP. Kindly ask most urgently ask American Government in my name to send ship to meet us and take us to New York STOP.*

The Brazilian then signed off by giving the ship's co-ordinates and without his customary good wishes or kind regards. The problem lay with a fault in the *Jeanne d'Arc*'s boilers which meant the vessel had lost power and was in danger of drifting. Though it does not seem as if the President-Elect and his family were in imminent danger, the incident clearly alarmed them. Fortunately a US ship, the *Imperator* – ironically a captured German vessel, heading home with more than 9,000 returning American troops on board – was in the area and was diverted to pick up the Brazilian delegation. The captain of the *Imperator* Casey Morgan later explained he had reached the *Jeanne D'Arc* at 1 o'clock in the morning. 'We ... found her dead still in the water ...' he recalled. The Brazilian presidential party was personally escorted by a senior US naval officer on the short but unnerving journey in small boats over the Atlantic waves and to the safety of the US vessel. 'The President enjoyed the tossing swell *en route* from the French cruiser a quarter of a mile away from us, but the women in the party were a little frightened. Some of the men didn't like the experience either,' the captain noted dryly. Meanwhile the stricken *Jeanne d'Arc* was towed to the Azores by another American ship. This was not the best of starts to his voyage, though it ended on a happier note. The *Imperator* was given an escort of US destroyers and received a 21-gun salute from Fort Wadsworth on Staten Island as the Brazilian delegation arrived at New York. Nor did Pessoa forget the two men whom he felt had been responsible for the rescue of himself and his party. The first was Captain Morgan, to whom he gave a signed photograph of himself. The other was the inventor Guglielmo Marconi, whose wireless telegraphy had allowed the French ship to call for help, and to whom he now sent a telegram praising the Italian's *marvellous invention*. The courteous and sometimes slightly formal Pessoa rarely forgot his manners.[8]

The President-Elect's first sight of the Manhattan skyline and the official greeting that awaited him had a profound impact on Epitácio. According to US officers on the *Imperator* he declared: *This is indeed the happiest day of my life.*

After braving a torrential downpour Pessoa and his entourage stayed at the Waldorf Astoria Hotel in New York before making their way on to Washington. It was overall a very successful and enjoyable trip for the Brazilian, despite his growing impatience to get back home. One small regret was that he was greeted in Washington by Vice-President Thomas Marshall rather than Woodrow Wilson. The President was of course still in Paris, waiting for the signing of the crucial treaty with Germany. The Brazilian was also slightly irked by the high degree of security that surrounded him. It was explained to him that he was thought to be at risk of assassination – though not because of who he was but because he bore a strong resemblance to Eamon de Valera, the prominent Irish politician who was in the United State from June 1919 trying to gain American recognition for the Irish Republic. Later in the trip, when staying again in New York, though this time at the Hotel Carleton, Pessoa slipped out of the hotel early one morning without his usual guards to go and explore the wonders of Fifth Avenue. He only got two blocks before there was a tug on his arm. It was Mr Nye, the head of his security detail. 'Mr. President, excuse me. I have strict orders from my government, I cannot consent to Your Excellency travelling without a guard,' he told him.[9]

This is indeed the happiest day of my life.
EPITÁCIO PESSOA

Half a world away in Paris, the Peace Conference was reaching another dramatic moment, if not quite its end. Relations between Clemenceau, Wilson and Lloyd George had become strained during the tense days before the signing of the German treaty, which had finally been earmarked for 28 June. Lloyd George had tried to renegotiate parts of the Treaty to make it slightly less unpalatable to the Germans, to the intense irritation of Clemenceau. Wilson, meanwhile, was annoyed by British and French moves to block any changes to the reparations clauses. As for the Germans, they had little choice but to sign, despite the deep anger back home. They did so reluctantly, and pointedly with their own pens. The curious ceremony took place in the Hall of Mirrors at Versailles, where each delegation – including the Brazilian one – queued up and signed the historic document. The first signature on behalf of the President of the Republic of Brazil was that of João Pandiá Calógeras, now officially head of the delegation in Epitácio's absence. Next came Raul Fernandes, whose relations with Pessoa had thawed slightly after their difficult start, and finally it was the turn of Rodrigo Octávio de L Menezes.

Brazil could at least claim to feature in the document, even if the majority of its terms dealt with boundaries and issues far removed from day to day South American concerns; Article 263 concerned its claim to the coffee that had been trapped in Germany. More importantly in terms of Brazil's future role in world affairs, it had been named on the first council of the League of Nations, one of the few tangible outcomes of the Treaty with overtly international implications. Though it had been criticised for its selfish, even mercenary approach to the Conference, Brazil had at least made a small but notable contribution to the League. It was a sign that the course set by Rio Branco towards a greater willingness to play a role on the world stage was still being followed.

Brazil's minor successes at the Conference were partly due to Pessoa's skilful negotiating, but also owed much to President Woodrow Wilson's willingness to help Brazil. In a sense the US helped create a role for Brazil on the world stage, a role it was to enjoy for a brief period. It was ironic then that before long the United States itself would be turning its back on the League and to some extent the world as it embarked on an era of isolationism. As for Epitácio Pessoa, finally heading home to take up his presidency, it would largely be domestic issues rather than foreign policy that would occupy his time in office.

Pessoa (2nd row, far left) at the inaugural session of the Permanent Court of International Justice.

III

The Legacy

7

Power and Problems: 1919–22

Epitácio Pessoa returned to the country of which he was now president in some style. After a brief stop in his home state of Paraíba, he arrived in Rio de Janeiro on 21 July 1919, having been out of the country for more than six months. The elaborate welcome ceremony had been arranged for some time, and included 5,000 girls – the daughters of local workers – being despatched on a fleet of vessels to greet the new president as he arrived aboard the *Idaho*. As a planning memo of the time reveals, this populist fleet then accompanied the new president's boat to the quay, from where he was escorted in a procession along Rio Branco Avenue. The streets were strewn with flowers 'that not only gladden the eye, but speak to one's spirit and heart', before the president was greeted at the palace by the ubiquitous 5,000 girls singing a workers' hymn in his honour.[1]

On his way back to Brazil, Pessoa had taken the time to thank President Wilson for the welcome he had received in the United States, and to underline once more the growing ties between the two countries. *I am ever more convinced that it is the duty of our two governments – already linked by a friendship that has become traditional – to strengthen as much as possible the relations between our two peoples ... it requires only that we get to know one another better ... showing the advantages that the two countries can offer each other ... please believe Your Excellency that this will be one of my dearest concerns.* For their part, American diplomats were convinced the Brazilian had been 'greatly impressed' by the 'power and energy' of the United States and that this boded well for future relations. He had also returned to Brazil in an American warship, symbolic of his strong links with that country during the Conference. However he admitted this was not his idea, and that he had tried to get out of it. *This causes me great embarrassment,* he told the Foreign Ministry.[2] But Pessoa now had to turn his attentions to domestic affairs. Brazil may have been on the fringes of the First World War and the subsequent Peace Conference, but nonetheless the war and its aftermath had caused considerable changes in the country.

> It is the duty of our two governments ... to strengthen as much as possible the relations between our two peoples
> EPITÁCIO PESSOA TO PRESIDENT WILSON

After the difficult period at the beginning of the war, Brazil's economy had performed well during the conflict and in 1919 coffee prices were high, prompting something of a mini-boom, while other crops such as cotton had also become important. At the same time, there were signs that Brazil, long dominated by agriculture, was beginning to develop a significant industrial sector. The 1890s had seen the first beginnings of industrial growth, mostly in São Paulo and the Federal District (i.e. Rio), much of it devoted to textiles and food processing – in other words, industries linked to agricultural production. Heavy industry was still relatively scarce, though shipbuilding was a growing sector. The war had certainly encouraged this industrial growth – developed economies in Europe were otherwise engaged and many imported products had become scarce. At the same time the war had also made business people and politicians in Brazil painfully aware of just how dependent they were on the rest of the world for key materials such as steel and coal. An example of this was the disputes Brazil had had with the US over coal imports during the war. Meanwhile cement, machinery and iron all had to be imported.

An important factor associated with growth in industry was the emergence of Brazil's urban working classes. Rebellion and unrest were well-known in the countryside, but during the war and immediately afterwards there was also unrest in the cities sparked by low wages and a rise in the cost of food. Some of the biggest disturbances occurred in São Paulo and Rio in June and July 1917, with the unrest spreading to other parts of the country. The authorities' handling of these protests followed what became a familiar pattern: using force to suppress trouble, while at the same time making some significant compromises on issues such as pay. There were also serious disturbances in May 1919 on the eve of Pessoa's return. Such protests were largely governed by local factors – such as food prices – but there was also an international dimension. The Bolshevik Revolution in Russia in 1917 had sent shockwaves not just through Europe (and the 1919 Peace Conference) but the rest of the world too. Thus May Day protests in cities such as Rio in 1918 and 1919 became a way of showing solidarity with the new workers' state far away.

However, there was never any serious threat of a Bolshevik-style workers' uprising in Brazil. For one thing trade union organisation was weak. In addition, the main aim of Brazilian workers – whose more radical elements tended to be anarchists rather than communists – was to improve their conditions rather than overthrow the system. Nonetheless this did not stop some sections of the government from fearing insurrection and seeking new powers to control the situation. A particular focus was on the number of alleged foreign agitators entering the country, and in 1919 President Pessoa warned the Foreign Ministry to take *the greatest care* when issuing visas. This was a time when many so-called White Russians were fleeing the country to seek a new home and the authorities feared Bolshevik agitators could join their ranks. In addition a number of foreign-born workers' leaders – immigrants were heavily involved in the trade union movement – were deported. Then in 1920 Pessoa and his government were granted new anti-subversion powers by Congress in a bid to control foreign agents *whose ideal is the abolition of the Fatherland, destruction of the family and banishment of all religion.* By late 1920, however, workers' protests fizzled out, largely because their relatively weak organisations were unable to resist the highly organised and harsh repression meted out to them. Nevertheless, they did leave a mark on Brazilian society. For the first time national politicians realised they needed to take account of the urban working classes.[3]

Another factor linked to the growth in industry was a rise in economic nationalism. Brazilians had noted how when national interest was at stake even supposed allies such as the United States, Britain and France would not hesitate to adopt policies that were against Brazil's interests. As a result, a desire to end its dependence on other countries became an important driver in the Brazil's industrial expansion over the coming years, with São Paulo at the forefront. Indeed, the war and the immediate post-war period was characterised by a more general awakening of national sentiment in Brazil. The war in Europe had shown that nationalism was still a potent force in the world, a sober reminder for any Brazilian who believed lofty internationalism had become the predominant force in world diplomacy. Brazilians also noted how, for all their supposed culture and heritage, the Old World countries had still managed to slip into the most bloody of wars. A growing if vague idea that the New World – the Americas – could exert growing moral and political leadership in the world began to take hold. The country was finally starting to lose the intellectual inferiority complex it had long suffered in relation to Europe.

President Pessoa was himself a strong nationalist. This was not despite his recent diplomatic experiences in Paris but partly because of them. He and his fellow delegates had seen at first hand the way smaller nations were treated by larger ones, and how international principles got pushed aside in the face of naked national self-interest. Indeed, one could argue that Pessoa's determination to drive the hardest of bargains over the coffee and ships issues – an approach that earned Brazil criticism in Paris – was simply a recognition of this diplomatic reality. Throughout the 1920s Brazilian diplomacy was dominated by a pragmatic and deeply cynical view of how the world worked. Domício da Gama, who under Pessoa lost his job as Foreign Minister and was made Ambassador to Britain, and who had watched the machinations in Paris from afar, noted that friendship between countries was no more than 'an artificial sentiment born of momentary convenience'. The problem was that for a nation to survive in such treacherous circumstances – as recent world events had shown – it needed to be able to defend itself. 'Nobody respects or seeks the solidarity of the weak,' noted Calógeras on his return from Paris. Yet at the end of the First World War Brazil's military was in a poor state.[4]

'The French officers have the worst opinion of the efficiency of the army …' was the damning verdict of a British diplomat in Rio de Janeiro. He was referring to the military mission that had been appointed at the end of the war to oversee improvements in the Brazilian army. It was not a huge success. In 1922 the French officer in charge of the operation, General Maurice Gamelin, pulled the plug on one set of manoeuvres in southern Brazil because of the 'complete disorientation' of the home army. Apparently troops were getting lost because their officers could not read maps or use a compass properly. The bemused French regarded their task as 'almost hopeless'. The navy was hardly in better shape and was regarded by the Americans as 'clearly inferior' to those of Chile and Argentina.[5]

It was a weakness that Pessoa was acutely aware of and during his time in office he warned Congress about the shortcomings of the country's armed forces. Moreover, he was determined his administration would at least start the process of reforming and strengthening the military. He appointed as War Minister a man who was committed to military reform – Calógeras. In many ways Calógeras was an excellent choice. Having just spent many months in Paris he had an intimate knowledge of international defence issues and a wide potential network of international contacts. The fact that he had been able to work closely with Pessoa was also a help. The problem was simply that Calógeras was a civilian – the first civilian, indeed, to have held the post of War Minister since the start of the Republic. Another civilian, Raul Soares, was made Navy Minister. The armed forces were not amused. From the moment Pessoa had announced his intentions to appoint Calógeras, rumours started to spread about how the military would react. The new president, however, stood firm – even when he was approached directly with what amounted to an ultimatum. *One of the most prestigious Generals in the Army advised me to overturn my decision in order to avoid an armed movement. I replied: 'Tomorrow, the press will publish the name of a civilian being appointed to the Navy Ministry.*

I will resist – and let us see who the nation backs.
EPITÁCIO PESSOA

I dare the Army, I mean, the rebels in the Army, to disturb the order of the Republic against the uncontestable right of the President to choose the person to command a government ministry. I will resist – and let us see who the nation backs.' The country chose to back the new president. However, this was the beginning of ill-feeling between Pessoa and the military that would lead to more significant clashes later in his presidency. Once more in Brazil the role of the armed forces in politics was becoming a major and divisive issue.[6]

Pessoa's desire to improve the armed forces, and especially the navy, was complicated by another factor – international disarmament. The question had been raised at Paris, most specifically in relation to Germany. Reducing a nation's armaments in line with its defensive needs had also been one of Woodrow Wilson's famous Fourteen Points in 1918. In 1921 the new US President Warren Harding organised a conference on naval disarmament in Washington. However, this was billed as a meeting of the Great Powers only and to its dismay Brazil was excluded. This was an irritating reminder of the way that Brazil and other nations had been treated at Paris. More important and complex however, was Brazil's reaction to the question of disarmament itself. In theory, and in keeping with its status as a member of the council of the League of Nations, Brazil was in favour of the idea. In practice, though, it feared disarmament would in effect simply preserve the *status quo* and thus maintain Brazil's position as a naval weakling in South America. With its long coastline and dependence on maritime trade, Brazil was always acutely aware of its potential vulnerability from the sea. And in particular it was worried about one of its neighbours – Argentina.

Brazil had long been wary of its regional rival to the south, but after the First World War its nervousness grew. Paradoxically, though it had not joined in the war, Argentina's military was in much better shape that Brazil's. Military assessments by foreign observers in the early 1920s suggested Argentina could raise three times as many trained troops as Brazil, and mobilise them more quickly too. Nor was Argentina content to rest there, for by 1927 its annual defence budget had tripled in comparison with that of 1919. It also both modernised its navy and extended the railway network, which the Brazilian authorities looked upon with alarm because they saw them as a rapid means of deploying troops. At the same time as it was increasing its own military strength, Argentina was also – cynically in Rio's eyes – warning about the supposed dangers of Brazil's armed forces and its regional ambitions. The arrival of the French Military Mission in Brazil had unnerved Buenos Aires, even if its impact was limited. Equally alarming was the fact that the US Navy won a contract in 1922 to help modernise the Brazilian navy. A senior Argentine foreign affairs official described Brazil as a serious menace, and though the two countries upgraded their diplomatic representation to ambassador level, the age-old tensions re-surfaced.

It was during this time that Brazilian military officers gave voice to their own misgivings about their country's security – or lack of it – in South America. As the only Portuguese-speaking country surrounded by Spanish-speaking ones, Brazil had a tendency to feel isolated, a suspicion that seems not to have diminished despite international meetings and regular pan-American gatherings. One naval commander bleakly described the country's position as one of 'complete isolation'. An army chief meanwhile noted: 'We are surrounded by nations who do not have the slightest sympathy for us, who are jealous of our prosperity and who cannot forgive our increasing development ...'. Inevitably the biggest threat was perceived to come from Argentina. One senior Brazilian military figure believed their Spanish-speaking neighbour was aiming for the 'diplomatic isolation of Brazil in South America ... '. Such threats meant that whatever its high-minded international idealism, Brazil found it impossible to accept any checks on increasing the strength of its navy to act in self-defence. As the Foreign Minister José Félix Alves Pacheco put it in 1923, Brazil could not accepts limits on the level of armament that was necessary to deal with a 'South American crisis'. He added, 'We cannot limit that of which we have too little.' Meanwhile, at an early meeting of the new League of Nations, a Brazilian delegate Rodrigo Octávio declared: 'We cannot give our consent to the proposal of not increasing, over the next two years, the current military budgets. Brazil is certainly a liberal and pacific country, with no imperialist or militarist tendencies. But its territory is considerable, its coastline very long and, for its domestic requirements, it is necessary to have an Army and Navy ...'[7]

It was against this backdrop of growing military unease – not helped by his own cabinet appointments and his vetoing of a pay rise for the military – that Epitácio Pessoa began to confront serious problems as president. Initially, he was a popular figure, who was perceived to have done his country good service at the Peace Conference and who had shown character in standing up to the military. The formal ratification of the Treaty of Versailles by Brazil was promulgated on 12 January 1920 and this, coupled with the official visit by the Belgian King Albert the same year, were welcome reminders of those successes at Paris. However, as Pessoa had feared, the short-lived economic boom soon ended; during 1920 the level of exports had fallen below imports, coffee prices had dropped and the exchange rate had moved against Brazil. To prop up the dominant coffee industry the federal government once more resorted to the old policy of buying and hoarding coffee, while the treasury borrowed more money. It was not long before political tensions rose as well.

Pessoa's surprise adoption as presidential candidate had been the result of conflicts within the ruling elite in Brazilian politics, splits that had not gone away with his election. By early 1921 it was time again in the political process for the act that always highlighted any political fault lines in national politics – the choosing of the next 'official' candidate. It was a process that was to sour the final two years of Epitácio Pessoa's presidency and underline how the informal power structures that held together the First Republic were beginning to crumble.

To kick off the election merry-go-round, two of the dominant states São Paulo and Minas Gerais nominated Artur Bernardes as their official candidate. He was the governor of Minas Gerais. However, the third state in the triumvirate, Rio Grande do Sul, led by Borges de Madeiros, strongly objected to the choice, and now bitterly criticised the old *café con leite* alliance and its approach to political selection in Brazil. Disquiet at the way that Brazilian politics and economics were dominated by coffee interests to the detriment of the overall economy had existed since the mid-1890s. But this open disagreement from a major state such as Rio Grande do Sul was a sign that it was growing. Other states from around the country, including Bahia and Pernambuco, now backed this opposition and joined together to form a loose coalition known as Republican Reaction. They chose as their alternative candidate Nilo Peçanha, who, having initially backed Bernardes for the presidency, now saw a chance to get the top job for himself. Disaffected sections of the military also allied themselves to this *ad hoc* coalition. It was a disparate grouping that had no radically alternative political platform to the 'official' politicians; in fact they were driven largely by personal rivalries and a sense of being excluded from power. Nonetheless Brazilian politics were becoming dangerously split and factionalised.

Military support for the Republican Reaction side grew in October 1921 when a Rio de Janeiro newspaper published an incendiary letter it said had fallen into its hands. The letter was said to have been written by Bernardes to a political ally. In it the presidential candidate made insulting remarks about the military. Unsurprisingly the contents provoked outrage among the military, even though it was clear to any objective observer the letter was an unsubtle forgery designed to make mischief. Their anger was increased still further when it was declared authentic by Rio de Janeiro's influential Clube Militar. This was now led by Marshal Hermes da Fonseca, who had returned from a long stay in Europe and who as a former head of state was a major figure around whom military opposition could coalesce.

The presidential elections that took place in March 1922 were remarkably peaceful in the circumstances. The fragile mood did not last long, though. Though the poll showed Bernardes had won by around 150,000 votes, the President-Elect was booed publicly in the streets of Rio. More seriously, the Republican Reaction coalition announced it did not accept the result while the increasingly strident Hermes called for a special court to rule on the fairness of the poll. He claimed he did not trust Congress to decide even though this was its constitutional duty. For a while Brazil appeared to teeter on the brink; would the military intervene? At a crisis meeting at the Palácio do Catete – the presidential palace – Pessoa and key ministers and politicians met to discuss the next step. They eventually decided to reject calls for a special court or commission and instead left it to Congress to validate the result, which it duly did. During the meeting Pessoa allegedly stated the situation would be better if Bernardes withdrew from the presidency – a remark he later denied having made. In the end nothing came of the idea and he publicly pledged to hand over power to Bernardes in November as planned. However, Bernardes later got to hear of the alleged remark and this cost Pessoa the goodwill of his successor.

Though the military hierarchy was still angry at the direction of the government and over Bernardes' election, they had held back from open revolt. But this was the first time in the First Republic they had been so estranged from the elected government, and they were determined to do all they could to undermine government authority. Their chance came during elections in Pernambuco when Pessoa was accused by opposition politicians of allowing federal troops to be used to favour one side – which just happened to include members of his family. Pessoa himself was blameless, though some of his relatives probably misused their influence to seek the help of troops in elections that were marred by riots, banditry and shootings. The president's critics, however, were certain Pessoa was behind the episode and Hermes himself telegraphed the local garrison in Recife urging them to disobey the government's orders. It was an extraordinary act of defiance from a man who was both a leading military figure and a former president of the Republic – one, moreover, who had watched over a number of interventions or 'salvations' in states when he was in power. In fact it was so extraordinary that Pessoa ordered his Minister of War to check with Hermes that the Marshal had really written the message. Hermes confirmed he had. Pessoa had little choice but to take action. After all, as he wrote later: *This telegram was not only a blow against discipline; it was an attack on the truth. The Marshal insinuated … that the President was illegally intervening in Pernambuco … .* When the military officer refused to accept a formal reprimand he was briefly arrested, and the Clube Militar was closed for six months. Defending himself later against criticism of the arrest, Pessoa said that to have meekly accepted Hermes' refusal to be reprimanded *would [have been] the government's end. The President's authority would disappear, to have been replaced by a disobedient and rebel general … only a mad person or a fanatic could see this attitude as an act of repression or personal retaliation.* Yet it would provide justification for a serious attack on the President's authority soon afterwards.[8]

The senior ranks of the military were furious at Hermes' treatment and the action against the Clube Militar. Yet they still they held back from open rebellion, unwilling to take that final, irrevocable step against the government. More junior officers, however, had fewer inhibitions. Many had become appalled by what they saw as the cynicism, weakness and corruption of government in Brazil. On 5 July 1922 a group of junior officers staged a revolt at Fort Copacabana in Rio de Janeiro, and were soon joined in their action by cadet officers at the Military Academy. The avowed aim of the rebellion was to restore the honour of the military, though it was unclear just how this was to be achieved. Crucially the senior officers remained loyal to the government and the fort came under bombardment. Seeing this, most of the young officers realised the revolt was finished and surrendered. But a small group of 18 of them continued the fight and most of them perished in a brief but bloody showdown on Copacabana beach.

Though the young officers had posed no real threat to Epitácio Pessoa's government, the legend of the heroic 'Copacabana 18' took on a life of its own. Out of this brave if futile protest was born the phenomenon of *tenentismo*. Epitácio himself blamed the revolt on *wicked politicians, militaries, and journalists moved by personal or political party interests.* For him the threat had felt like a real and a serious one. *Every patriot can imagine the terror that would have occurred if [the revolt] had triumphed: the military dictatorship, weak and incapable, oppressing the freedom; our reputation lost on the international scene; the splits, the Bolshevism ... .* [9]

The rise of *tenentismo* was just one sign of a changing mood in Brazilian society. Until then, the main radical trend within the labour movement had been anarchism, which had at first drawn strength from the Bolshevik Revolution. However, the movement split over differences on how to react to developments in Russia, and in March 1922 the Brazilian Communist Party was formed, which closely followed the Moscow line. The Catholic Church, too, was undergoing change, with leaders supporting the creation of new organisations to help provide education and healthcare for the working classes. This once again reflected the growing importance and scale of the urban classes. Among intellectuals as well, there was a discernible shift in Brazil away from Eurocentric thought towards a more authentic Brazilian way of looking at the world. This found concrete form in the three festivals for music, visual arts and literature held in São Paulo in February 1922 and known collectively as the Modern Art Week. The participants, who included Pessoa's old classmate Graça Aranha, publicly rejected what they saw as the moribund, backward-looking, and European-dominated cultural scene and demanded a more modern approach with Brazil's uniquely varied society as its centrepiece.

Amid this changing world, Epitácio Pessoa ended his presidency on 15 November, an angry and slightly bewildered man. A profound patriot, he had done what he thought best for his country, trying to control spending, supporting projects to help alleviate the perennial problems of drought in the north-east, respecting the constitution and trying to modernise the military while at the same time refusing to give way to their political demands. Yet he faced criticism over the weakening state of the economy, over allegations that he had abused power to help his family and for

TENENTISMO
The phenomenon of the *tenentes* – literally lieutenants or junior officers – was born in 1922 and had an important psychological significance out of proportion to their actual achievements. Their revolts and famous march known as the Prestes Column brought little concrete change but showed that the decentralised oligarchic system could be challenged at the barrel of a gun – and this was how the First Republic indeed fell in 1930. The *tenentes*' ideology was short on detail, but was nationalistic, corporatist and supported education of the people. Self-styled saviours of the nation, a key aim was the removal of the oligarchic system they felt was corrupt and damaging to the country's interests.

his supposed failure to deal with military grievances. The problem was partly one of generation. Pessoa looked like, and indeed was, an old-fashioned oligarch; someone at home with the political balancing act of the First Republic, the tight control of power in the states weighed against the growing demands of central government. This old way of doing things was slowly starting to break down however as new groups jostled to make their voices heard. The First World War had provided a brake on changes in society, but once war was over the clamour for change had grown. Pessoa represented the past. More and more Brazilians desired something new.

8
Last Days of the Republic: 1922–30

Throughout his adult life Epitácio Pessoa had spent considerable time in Europe, whether on holiday, honeymoon or for his career. So it was no great surprise that when his brief term of office as president came to an end in November 1922, it was Europe that beckoned once more. First he took a lengthy trip abroad. Then in August 1923 and in recognition of his legal credentials and in keeping with his country's continuing desire to have a role on the global scene, Pessoa was nominated as one of the judges sitting at the Permanent Court of International Justice (PCIJ) in the Hague.

In many ways it was an ideal posting for Pessoa after his difficult time as president. For one thing, thanks partly to his indiscreet comment at the Catete, for the first time in many years he was now on bad terms with the current head of state. This would have blocked progress in any domestic political career he might have pursued, but was of less concern in The Hague. The judicial posting was moreover a role for which he was intellectually and temperamentally well suited. Thirdly it was a sufficiently prestigious posting to satisfy his undoubted vanity, having just served as head of the Paris peace delegation and then president. Finally, Europe was a place where he felt happy and at home, and was a culture he understood well. Apart from the Hague and Paraíba, the former president and his wife Mary spent much of their time at his favourite hotel in the Tuscan spa town of Montecatini, a place he adored. It was perhaps telling that this old-fashioned oligarch of Brazilian politics should be based in Europe just as Brazil itself – or at least its intelligentsia – was beginning to explore its South American identity and explicitly turning its back on old cultural ties. Yet if Pessoa was now no longer centre-stage in Brazilian national politics, he had not entirely retired from the fray. From the sedate surrounds of the Hague he kept in close touch with events in Paraíba where *Epitacismo* was still the prominent force in state politics and from where he oversaw the appointment and election of key people. In fact it was his desire to keep control of the choice of governor that briefly brought the ageing lawyer back into national politics, and for a while set him on a potentially dangerous collision course with President Bernardes.

THE INTERNATIONAL COURT IN THE HAGUE
The Permanent Court of International Justice (PCIJ), as it was officially titled, was established under Article 14 of the Covenant of the League of Nations and though it was legally separate from that body, the two worked closely together. It was a body with which Epitácio Pessoa was already familiar, having been on the commission that drew up the League. It contained ten leading jurists from around the world and first sat in February 1922; it was intended to be a place where disputing nations could obtain an authoritative ruling over the issues that divided them. At the end of the Second World War, it was replaced by a new International Court of Justice.

In 1924 the outgoing governor of the north-eastern state, Solon de Lucena, chose as his successor João Suassuna, a candidate endorsed by Pessoa himself. However, not all factions within the wider Pessoa clan were happy about the choice, and they took their complaints to the president in Rio. It was a shrewd move, given President Bernardes' somewhat strained relations with Epitácio. President Bernardes had already moved quickly to cut funding for the projects his predecessor had set up to help alleviate the north-east's perennial drought problems. With Pessoa no longer president, these schemes were always vulnerable to a lack of political support in Rio, and President Bernades had no desire to continue a policy that helped his predecessor's reputation but not his own. The dissident faction's justification for their complaints – that Suassuna had been involved in some suspect deals involving the drought relief programme – therefore struck a particular chord with the president. This was a dangerous time for Pessoa. Bernardes made it clear if the name of Pessoa's candidate was on the ballot, he would carry out what was known as a 'beheading' or removal of the candidate from the list. Such a public rebuke would dangerously weaken Pessoa's control in his state.

A worried Pessoa left The Hague in the late spring of 1924 and hastened to Rio de Janeiro. Here, thanks to his influence with the current state Governor Solon, he was able to sit in Congress as a Paraíban senator. He used this position as a national platform to defend the nomination of Suassuna to be Paraíba's governor, in the knowledge that if he failed his power in the state would be damaged – perhaps permanently. Fortunately two factors conspired to save him from losing face. One was his own capability to negotiate with rival factions. During the course of the Brazilian winter he managed to persuade key opponents of his protégé's candidature to withdraw their formal objections. The second, and probably more important, factor was an outbreak of violent unrest in Brazil that occupied all of President Bernardes' attention and meant the removal of Suassuna did not take place. Ironically the unrest that helped save Pessoa's grip on Paraíba came from the same source that he had confronted as president in 1922: army lieutenants.

The revolt started in mid-1924, timed to mark the second anniversary of the doomed but heroic Copacabana incident. Once again the rebellion was led by young army officers – the 'lieutenants' – though this time they had a veteran officer in charge, General Isidoro Dias Lopes. The rebellion started in São Paulo and unlike the previous episode was both well-organised and had a very specific aim: to overthrow President Bernardes and with him the hated oligarchy. In reality, the relatively small group of officers involved had little real hope of achieving their goals. But neither did they surrender when their position looked hopeless. Three weeks after starting the revolt, and having come under attack from loyal troops, the rebels escaped from São Paulo and headed south into neighbouring Paraná state. Here they planned to link up with another rebel group, this one from Rio Grande do Sul. Elsewhere there were mini-rebellions too, notably in Belém and Manaus, and the crew of the battleship *São Paolo* mutinied and sailed for Uruguay and exile. But it was the officers from São Paolo and Rio Grande do Sul who formed the heart of the rebellion. The southern section was led by a Captain Luis Carlos Prestes, and it was he who lent his name to the extraordinary event that was to follow.

Unable to achieve their aims, the so-called Prestes Column of rebels set off on a remarkable and gruelling 24,000-km journey that lasted until March 1927 and which took in many of Brazil's remote backlands. The aim of this column – which probably never numbered more than 1,500 at any one time – was to foment rebellion in Brazil's countryside, something it signally failed to do. Eventually it petered out, and its weary members sought refuge across the border in Bolivia and Paraguay. Yet despite the revolt's clear failure, the officers' efforts had an impact on Brazil. While the soldiers had not tapped into the considerable urban discontent that existed in many of the big cities, their self-sacrifice served as an example of how the country could be saved from what was seen as its current malaise and underlined that there were people willing to fight for it. In particular, the figure of Prestes, who became known as the Knight of Hope, enjoyed heroic status among sections of society. In practice the political aims of those who marched in the Prestes Column were quite vague, amounting to little more than wanting to renew the country and rid it of its self-interested oligarchs. This vagueness is hardly surprising given that Captain Prestes himself had no clear idea of what he wanted to achieve. 'I was merely a man disgusted with the way the country was governed,' he admitted at the time. After the column ended its march Prestes was introduced to Marxism and later became a communist, splitting with many of his fellow lieutenants along the way.[1]

The turmoil in Brazil caused by the July 1924 revolt may have helped Pessoa's cause in Paraíba, but it also made the country an unsafe place for the former president, who had faced down the earlier rebellion in 1922. By now back in Europe, Pessoa, a devoted family man, was once more contemplating a holiday in Brazil to see his daughters. However, his friends and family urged him to delay his planned return in October, fearing his life was at risk. For his daughters' sake he agreed to stay away despite the *homesickness* he admitted suffering. Instead he and Mary spent the autumn travelling in Egypt, where they saw the Pyramids, before returning once more to the Italian Riviera. Meanwhile one of his daughters had telegraphed saying it was safe to return, so Pessoa now decided to leave for home. He was still worried his life might be at risk, but even more concerned that his family would feel guilty about asking him to return should anything happen to them. Anxious to put their minds at rest, he penned a valedictory letter to one of his daughters before the ship docked at Rio: *Do not regret giving me your opinion to return home: even without the telegram I received in Cairo ... I would have come back. It was an unshakable resolution. I am not telling you this as a consolation, I swear to you it's true. As a comfort to the loss you face today, do not forget, as your mother and sisters – who are victims too – should not forget, that I was a dignified and a happy man, full of blessings and gifts ... Kindest Regards, my little daughter, with all the tenderness you can imagine, Papa.*

This moving letter remained locked away in Pessoa's possessions and was only found by his family after his death.[2]

On his emotional return in December 1924 Pessoa brought back more with him than a secret message of his love for his family; he also had with him the nearly-completed manuscript of a book he was compiling. It was published soon afterwards as *Pela Verdade*. Its aim was to tell the truth (*verdade*) about his presidency and to answer the many accusations made against him. It was an extraordinary and unprecedented book for a Brazilian politician to produce and the decision to write it at all gives a profound insight into his character. His pride, arrogance and his sense of doing the right thing simply could not allow him to miss the opportunity to correct what he saw as unjust criticism. To have stayed silent would have offended the lawyer in him. Much of the

> **I was a dignified and a happy man, full of blessings.**
> EPITÁCIO PESSOA

criticism concerned the taking out of loans by the Brazilian government while he was in charge – and which Pessoa now justified in great detail. One of the loans was for £9 million and was raised to buy stocks of coffee when prices fell – part of the so-called valorisation process that had occurred for many years in Brazil. Critics claimed there was nothing left of the loan, but in *Pela Verdade* an aggrieved Pessoa pointed out that the coffee the loan had bought was still in stock. *This loan can be considered as the best financial operation ever done in Brazil so far. The national economy has profited to the tune of more than four million Contos so far ...*, insisted the former president.[3]

The book created considerable controversy in Brazil, and inevitably attracted more criticism for its author. His daughter Laurita believed the book was brought out earlier than he had planned because of the hostility towards him from elements of the Bernardes government. In a letter to his daughter from The Hague in 1925 Pessoa showed that he almost relished the fight, and was anxious to get back to Brazil to answer his critics in person. Showing characteristic self-confidence in his debating and intellectual prowess he wrote: *You ask me, what is going to happen when I am back? When I am back, the flame will switch on again ... I will be able to conduct the defence in person, so certain critics will not dare to speak up. After all, not all of these combats displease me, especially when I can speak with a superiority that my opponents do not have ...*[4] And true to his word he used his seat in Congress to defend himself with some feisty speeches in October 1925.

> **Not all of these combats displease me, especially when I can speak with a superiority that my opponents do not have.**
> EPITÁCIO PESSOA

As Pessoa's difficulties suggest, Brazil under Bernardes was a tough, authoritarian place. The semi-reclusive president sought and received extra powers to deal with the unrest, including restrictions on the press. Declarations of states of siege in the country were commonplace. However, his economic policies did help bring some of the inflation that had developed under Pessoa under control, and this, combined with a more favourable world market for coffee, allowed the economy to recover some of its post-war buoyancy. The result was that by 1926 Bernardes was in a strong enough position to hand power to his chosen successor in relative peace. This smooth transition of power was helped by the fact that the key states had this time managed to agree on the official candidate, Washington Luís Pereira de Sousa, a 'Paulista' from São Paulo who had actually been born in the state of Rio de Janeiro. Washington Luís, a more cheerful character than Bernades, also managed to lift the country's mood by removing press restrictions and public order clampdowns.

Yet though it looked rather like business as usual in the Catete, appearances were deceptive. Brazil was changing. The veteran Rui Barbosa, who had been in the first government of the new republic and who had been a continual presence on the Brazilian political scene ever since, had died in 1923, his demise marking the end of an era. Meanwhile, in 1926 a new political party called the Partido Democrático was formed in São Paulo state; it had a relatively liberal programme and was supported by the growing professional classes.

There were signs, too, that Brazilians were not just starting to re-examine their cultural identity but their racial identity too. The prevailing racial theory in Brazilian thought was that the country's population would gradually 'whiten', a phenomenon regarded as something to be welcomed. This view continued well into the 1920s and 1930s. What changed was the hitherto often unquestioned assumption that Brazil's mixed racial heritage was a bad thing. In the 1920s, though more especially the 1930s, a handful of Brazil's social scientists and intellectuals began to focus on the country's African heritage. Until then focus on the country's blacks had mostly been in the context of slavery. Now the anthropologist Edgar Roquette-Pinto, the sociologist Gilberto Freyre and others began to examine the nation's African heritage and its contribution to what it was to be Brazilian. It was a slow process and one that would have to compete against rival theories of Aryan superiority prevalent in European thought at the time. But slowly Brazilian society – or at least sections of it – was starting to recognise its unique racial melting-pot was something to celebrate rather than denigrate.

Change of a rather more tangible kind occurred in Brazil's foreign status during this period, thanks largely to President Bernardes' obstinacy and his poor handling of diplomatic issues. Ever since Pessoa and Domício da Gama had used US backing to engineer the country a place on the League of Nation's permanent council, its status on the Geneva-based organisation had been a source of pride to Brazil's diplomats and politicians, and even the wider public. The fact that it was, initially at least, the only South American country on the council served to underline the nation's pre-eminent position in the region. The United States was not on the council, Washington having chosen to follow a path of isolation on the world stage. In Brazilian eyes, however, America's absence simply made Brazil's own status all the greater as the representative of the Americas.

For President Bernardes and his administration what mattered most was the fact of Brazil sitting on the League of

Nations council rather than the minutiae of policy and the League's actions. He regarded the details of European boundary disputes and the competing claims of different European peoples as largely unimportant to the national interest, and feared that becoming involved in them might actually harm Brazil's interests. What counted was being on the council, even if its influence there compared with countries such as Britain and France was slight. The problem was that Brazil was only a temporary member and this coveted place at the top table was subject to re-election. What Brazil really coveted was a permanent place on the council, a policy that soon became the Foreign Ministry's 'principal aspiration' under Bernardes and Foreign Minister Félix Pacheco. The latter believed that Brazil should be able to occupy the seat left vacant by Washington's absence. The issue was ducked in 1923 when the League voted to increase the council's Latin American representation to two, with both Brazil and Uruguay voted on for three years. But France and Britain were never receptive to the idea, and when Brazil once more pushed for permanent council status in 1925 it received a cool response. Referring to the 1924 revolt and the Prestes Column in Brazil, one British diplomat suggested 'the country is hardly being governed at all'. Another British observer, Sir John Tilley, perceptively described Brazil's real motivation at the time. This was, he believed, to be 'playing a showy part' in Geneva. He said if it failed in its attempt to get a permanent seat on the League of Nations council then Brazil's interest in the organisation would 'rapidly' wane.[5]

President Bernardes' actions were to prove Sir John right. Ignoring the advice from his own officials in Geneva to show more caution, the president adopted a high risk all-or-nothing strategy with the other members of the League council in late

1925 and early 1926. A key issue at the time – and certainly far more important to most council members – was the suggestion that Germany should be allowed onto the League's council. Brazil had no principled objection to this as long as it too was allowed to become a permanent member. So the Brazilian ambassador to the League, Melo Franco, was instructed to veto Germany's accession to the council if Brazil was not given what it wanted. For the president, national pride was now at stake and had to be maintained at any cost. But, as Melo Franco knew would happen, Britain and France ignored this attempt to force their hand and simply adjourned the council in March 1926, pending further elections later in the year. The implication was clear; Brazil would not only not be made a permanent council member, it would not be re-elected as a temporary member either, and as a result would lose its power of veto.

A distraught Melo Franco loyally carried out his country's symbolic but now meaningless veto at the council's final pre-adjournment meeting on 17 March. According to one account it was a remarkable spectacle: 'In the dead silence of the Assembly, pale, trembling, in tears even, he made his statement announcing that the Brazilian Government was resolved not to yield. Before this assembly of 48 nations, before a body of political leaders from almost every country in the world, the words uttered by the Brazilian delegate fell one by one like stones into a bottomless abyss.' The perceived slight to Brazilian pride provoked some demonstrations in Rio de Janeiro, and even persuaded President Bernardes to make a rare public appearance to defend his policy. Meanwhile, behind the scenes Brazilian diplomats tried to persuade European and American officials to come to Brazil's rescue. However, thanks to his clumsy and bullish diplomacy, Bernardes had pushed his country into a corner from which there was no escape and in June 1926 Brazil bowed to the inevitable and announced its decision to leave the League altogether, to avoid the inevitable further humiliation of failing to be re-elected to the council. It then gave orders to close its League of Nations office in Geneva and ordered most of its staff to return. When Pessoa heard the news in the Hague, his first instinct was to quit his position as a judge, out of loyalty to his country if not Bernardes. As he wrote to his daughter: *Not wanting to take such a grave decision on my own, I informed the government about my idea. Ten days later, it replied to me – in the negative.*[6]

Largely thanks to Bernardes' intransigence Brazil had been humiliated on the world stage. Bizarrely, the government tried to soften the blow a little by suggesting that the United States – who had never joined the council – congratulated Brazil on its actions. But even this desperate tactic backfired when the US formally denied it. Though the US now saw the League as largely a European organisation, it had no desire to undermine it. A number of diplomats and politicians in Brazil itself were furious. The lawyer, politician and future government minister José Carlos Macedo de Soares, writing soon afterwards, attacked the 'incredible follies' and blunders of the government adding, '… we do not realise how much we have suffered through the unprincipled policy of our public men in international diplomacy, on the greater stage of the world'. At one stroke a place at the top table of world politics – the one tangible benefit that Pessoa and his team had won for Brazil in the Treaty of Versailles save for the narrow issues of coffee and ships – had been thrown away. She had also made herself wretchedly isolated, gaining limited sympathy but no practical help from the US, and being abandoned in Geneva by fellow South American countries as well as the European powers. Even worse, she had done all that for no gain.[7]

The practical effects of Brazil's withdrawal from the League were not dramatic, given the organisation's focus on European issues and Brazil's limited involvement in such affairs. But it was a blow to national pride and reduced its prestige, undermining the more internationalist policy it had adopted since the days of Rio Branco and continued in Paris. In the space of just seven short years Brazil had gone from centre stage to the wings of international politics. The result of this bungled diplomacy was that in the following years, up to the Second World War, Brazil adopted a more narrowly focused foreign policy. Though less self-consciously isolationist that the United States, Brazil did not get involved in non-local international political issues until it felt compelled to do so – once again on the Allied side – when in a short period in August 1942 five of its ships were torpedoed and sunk by a single German submarine. In the meantime Brazil's main aims were to maintain good relations with the United States and play a prominent role in Latin American politics while keeping a wary eye on its powerful neighbour to the south. Its policy was fairly well summed up before the Havana Conference of 1928 when the Foreign Minister Octávio Mangabeira instructed his delegation to show the Americans Brazil was their friend in South America, while at the same time not falling out with Argentina. As part of the policy to keep Argentina in check, Brazil also sought to improve communications both diplomatically and literally with Paraguay and Bolivia two key countries squeezed between the two regional powers.

Yet if Brazil had made an unnecessary mess of its foreign policy, at home the country seemed to be heading for the end

a moment extirpate vices ingrained for years and years. You should act skilfully ... little by little, in order to avoid colliding violently with the [coroneis].[8]

The hotly-contested election was already underway in the autumn of 1929 when the Wall Street Crash occurred and sent shockwaves through the continent and around the world. By the time the election took place in March 1930 expectations of change were high. However, despite or perhaps because of the economic crisis looming in the coffee industry the official Paulista candidate Júlio Prestes was declared the winner, claiming more than 950,000 of the 1.5 million votes cast. Many factions within the Liberal Alliance cried foul, though after the obligatory protests about corruption Getúlio Vargas himself accepted the result.

But events in the north-east of Brazil then took a dramatic and fateful turn. Inside the wider Pessoa clan in Paraíba there were already deep divisions, with some of Epitácio's nephews siding with President Washington Luís against João Pessoa. Epitácio showed his displeasure and his ruthless streak by informing one of them: *You no longer exist for me.*[9] Meanwhile, João Pessoa had failed to heed his uncle's earlier wise advice about acting cautiously and had continued his tough campaign against banditry and political opponents in Paraíba. This provoked armed rebellion in the state and the beleaguered governor was looking likely to run short of arms and ammunition. In an extraordinary gesture of family loyalty, Epitácio, who was then in the Hague, arranged for ammunition to be smuggled by sea into Paraíba, concealing it in tins of fruit. But in his zeal João Pessoa had also mortally offended an opponent in the state and on 26 July this man took his revenge by gunning down the governor and vice-presidential candidate in the streets of

Recife. The murder of João Pessoa was the spark that relit the flames of opposition in the country, especially when the dead man's body was taken to Rio de Janeiro for a martyr's funeral. A distraught Epitácio Pessoa and others in Paraíba knew the young man had been killed for reasons of personal revenge rather than national politics. But this fact was lost or concealed in the outpouring of national anger and the blame for the killing was laid at the door of Washington Luís and his allies. In neighbouring Argentina, meanwhile, a military-backed coup overthrew President Hipólito Yrigoyen on 6 September and this too stoked up the mood of tension and rebellion inside Brazil.

The armed rebellion broke out in Paraíba, Minas Gerais and Rio Grande on 3 October. It involved some *tenentismo* officers, though hitherto loyal army units quickly joined in as the unrest spread. With the rebels soon poised to seize the strategically vital São Paulo state the military high command bowed to the inevitable and took charge of events itself. The army deposed the president on 24 October, and established a military junta. For a brief moment it looked as if the military were intent on staying in power. But on 31 October Getúlio Vargas made a timely arrival in Rio, wearing his trademark gaucho hat and greeted by cheering crowds. The military quickly handed over power to him as head of the provisional government. Though the military had been crucial to the overthrow of Washington Luís, the next regime was to be headed by a civilian.

Getúlio Vargas was a political insider of the First Republic and certainly no revolutionary. He took advantage of rather than shaped the events that led to his taking power. Nonetheless his arrival at head of the country signalled an end to the First Republic and the start of a new era in Brazilian politics. Vargas remained in power until 1945, first as head of the provisional government, then as president elected by Congress and finally from 1937 as dictator of what was called the *Estado Novo* or New State. He was elected president by the people for the first time in 1950, before his suicide in 1954. Domestically Vargas reduced the direct political influence of the coffee lobby though coffee remained a crucial element of the economy, increased the process of industrialisation and gave some concessions to the country's urban working classes, though subject to strict controls on, for example, industrial action.

In terms of foreign policy, the early Vargas years were dominated by the lead-up to the Second World War and the war itself. Here there were similarities with the First Republic and its reaction to the First World War. The strong economic ties with a resurgent Germany, and in some cases political sympathies too, at one point threatened to pull Brazil into the Axis camp. However, the lure of United States trade and offers of assistance proved an even stronger attraction. Moreover, pro-American factions recalled the lessons of the First World War and argued Brazil had far more to gain from being on the US and Allies' side. Brazil may have committed diplomatic suicide in 1926 but when war loomed, the lesson of 1917 – that Brazil was better off engaged rather than staying aloof – had been learnt. Brazil therefore followed the US's example when it broke off diplomatic relations with the Axis Powers in January 1942, and declared war seven months later, after losing five ships in three days to German submarines. This time Brazil's ground troops played an active role in the fighting, 25,000 men being sent to Italy in late 1944. In all, 451 lost their lives. Such action showed Brazil was once more a leading power in Latin America and helped it play a role in the new international organisation set up at the end of the war: the United Nations. After some years of self-induced isolation, Brazil was back in the international fold just as it had been at Paris in 1919.

Meanwhile, the murder of his impetuous but much-loved nephew hit Epitácio Pessoa hard. He received news of the attack while he was in his room at the Des Indes Hotel in The Hague. When his daughter Laurita, who was visiting at the time, saw him two hours later he looked so poorly that at first she assumed he had been taken ill. In some ways João Pessoa had been the son Epitácio never knew, a replacement for the infant who died in childbirth many years before. This traumatic act, just as much as the changing political scene in Brazil, marked a watershed for Pessoa, who was now 65 years old. He wanted to leave public life, and shortly after his nephew's death he gave up his candidacy for re-election to the International Court.

Back in Brazil, where he continued to work as a lawyer in private practice, Pessoa looked on at the increasingly authoritarian nature of the Vargas regime with quiet horror. The old *status quo* of the First Republic, its constitution and the admittedly clumsy way it had balanced powers and rights between central government and the states were being swept away. Back in 1929 Pessoa had supported the Liberal Alliance without ever really believing it would win at the ballot box, in which he was proved correct. But he had not foreseen the changes the arrival of Vargas in power heralded, which included the end of old-style oligarchic politics and in Paraíba the end of Pessoa's own political control. Local families still continued to have influence, but Vargas's government intervened directly in state politics as the power and reach of the central government grew. Friends and allies urged the former president to intervene publicly but Pessoa felt he had nothing in common with the new politics of Brazil and its new politi-

There is nothing more I can do for the country.
EPITÁCIO PESSOA

cians. *I do not speak the language of these people. I do not understand them, they do not understand me. There is nothing more I can do for the country*, he said. Later, as the 1930s wore on and Pessoa viewed the authoritarian governments existing in Europe, he was privately scathing about the powers Vargas had assumed. *Even in Germany, in fascist Italy, there always coexists a parliament, a representative body to satisfy the people's democratic desires. However, here, there is not even this. Everything depends on one man's decision!*[10]

In 1936 Pessoa, accompanied by Mary, got a chance to see at first hand the reality of Nazi Germany when they visited Berlin and witnessed the preparations for the Olympic Games there. The couple were also in Paris for the Bastille Day celebrations and later took in Belgium and Holland. It was the last time he visited his beloved Europe. On the way back to Rio the former president stopped off in Recife and visited the familiar streets where he had grown up and spent four years as a hard-working law student. But by now his health was beginning to fade. In 1936 he was diagnosed as suffering from Parkinson's Disease, and in 1937 he nearly died after suffering heart problems.

As the Second World War began Pessoa, who had abandoned the anti-clericalism of his youth and had now embraced the Catholic faith, was horrified at the reports of the atrocities that were coming from Europe. From his viewpoint they were a denial of the law and rights he had always fought for, including at the now distant Paris Peace Conference. According to his daughter Laurita: 'He could not accept that in a civilized world – in a world of freedom and rights, his world – such wartime actions could be carried out.'[11] He lived long enough to witness Brazil's ending of diplomatic relations with Germany, though not the declaration of war. Epitácio Pessoa died at his home at Petrópolis, near Rio de Janeiro, on 13 February 1942 at the age of 76. But his political age, the age of the First Republic and the rule of the oligarchs, had already ended more than a decade earlier.

Notes

1: Creation of the Republic: 1889–1900

1. Thomas E Skidmore, *Black into White: Race and Nationality in Brazilian Thought* (Duke University Press, Durham and London: 1993) pp 18–19, 92.
2. For a detailed account, see José Maria Bello, *A History of Modern Brazil 1889–1964* (Stanford University Press, Stanford: 1966) pp 52–5.
3. Bello, p 96.
4. *Perfis Parlamentares 7: Epitácio Pessoa* (Camara dos Deputados, Brasilia: 1978) pp 187–9.

2: Order and Progress: 1900–10

1. Linda Lewin, *Politics and Parantela in Paraíba: A case study of family-based oligarchy in Brazil* (Princeton University Press, Princeton: 1987) p 252.
2. *Obras Completas de Epitácio Pessoa* (Instituto Nacional do Livro, Rio de Janeiro: 1956) Vol 2, pp 255–6.
3. Joseph Smith, *Unequal Giants: Diplomatic Relations Between the United States and Brazil, 1889–1930* (University of Pittsburgh, Pittsburgh: 1991) p 63.

4. E Bradford Burns (ed), *A Documentary History of Brazil* (Knopf, New York: 1966) p 325.

3: The Republic Unravels: 1910–17
1. Bello, pp 216 and 223.
2. Lewin, p 301.
3. Lewin, pp 309–10; Fernando Melo, *Epitácio Pessoa: Uma Biografia* (Idéia João Pessoa: 2005) pp 78–9.
4. Bello, p 222.
5. Percy Alvin Martin, *Latin America and the War* (John Hopkins, Baltimore: 1925) pp 73–4; Frederick C Luebke, *Germans in Brazil* (Louisiana State University Press, Baton Rouge: 1987) p 75.
6. Luebke, p 93.

4: Brazil at War: 1917–18
1. Martin, p 78; Smith, p 99.
2. Martin, p 48.
3. Martin, pp 49–50.
4. Martin, pp 52–3.
5. Martin, pp 52–3; Smith, p 114.
6. Luebke, pp 111–13, 150.
7. Martin, pp 77–8; Luebke, pp 156–61.
8. Martin, p 20; Luebke, pp 162–74.
9. Martin, p 96; Luebke pp 200 and 196.
10. Martin, pp 97–8.
11. Lewin, p 307.
12. Melo, pp 75–7.
13. Melo, pp 75–7; Lewin, pp 316–17.

5: Paris 1919

1. Telegram from the Embassy in Washington to the Minister of Foreign Affairs on 24 November 1918, Ministério das Relações Exteriores (1916–1919) AHI 273–2-11 Conferência da Paz.

2. Charles W Turner, *Ruy Barbosa: Brazilian Crusader for the Essential Freedoms* (Abingdon-Cokebury, New York: 1945) p 162.

3. See for example Smith, p 126.

4. Melo, p 120.

5. Smith, p 127.

6. Smith, p 128.

7. Smith, p 128.

8. *Obras Completas*, Vol 14, p 7.

9. *Obras Completas*, Vol 14, p 8.

10. Telegram from the delegation in Paris to the Ministry of Foreign Affairs on 7 December 1918, Ministério das Relações Exteriores (1916–1919) AHI 273–2-11 Conferência da Paz; *Obras Completas*, Vol 14, p 8.

11. *Obras Completas*, Vol 14, p 8.

12. *Obras Completas*, Vol 14, p 11.

13. See Alan Sharp, *The Versailles Settlement: Peacemaking in Paris, 1919* (Macmillan, London: 1991) Chapter 2.

14. *Obras Completas*, Vol 14, pp 14–15.

15. *Obras Completas*, Vol 14, p 12; Laurita Pessoa Raja Gabaglia, *Epitácio Pessoa* (José Olympio, São Paulo: 1951) p 289; Edward Mandell House and Charles Seymour, *What Really Happened at Paris: The Story of the Peace Conference 1918–1919* (Charles Scribner's, New York: 1921) p 408.

16. *Obras Completas*, Vol 14, pp 14–15.

17. Smith, pp 130–1 and p 254.

18. *Obras Completas*, Vol 14, pp 14–15
19. See Smith, pp 128–33 on reaction to Brazil at the Conference. After the Conference a German protest saw the interest rate reduced to 4.5 per cent.
20. Smith, pp 130–1; Martin, pp 101–5; *Obras Completas*, Vol 14, p 34.
21. Smith, p 130; *Obras Completas*, Vol 14, p 34.
22. *Obras Completas*, Vol 14, p 14; Gabaglia, p 292.

6: From Delegate to President: April–June 1919

1. Melo, p 117; *Obras Completas*, Vol 14, pp 73–4.
2. Gabaglia, p 293.
3. *Obras Completas*, Vol 14, p 72.
4. *Obras Completas*, Vol 14, p 74.
5. *Obras Completas*, Vol 14, p 79.
6. *Obras Completas*, Vol 14, pp 38–40.
7. *Obras Completas*, Vol 14, p 18.
8. *Obras Completas*, Vol 14, pp 36, 20, 64; *New York Times*, 21 June 1919.
9. *New York Times*, 21 June 1919; Gabaglia, p 314.

7: Power and Problems: 1919–22

1. Archivo Paulo de Frontin, reference DL 1195.063; Smith, p 131.
2. *Obras Completas*, Vol 14, pp 23–6.
3. Stanley E Hilton, *Brazil and the Soviet Challenge 1917–1947* (University of Texas, Austin: 1991) pp 16 and 19.
4. Stanley E Hilton, 'Brazil and the Post-Versailles World: Elite Images and Foreign Policy Strategy, 1919–1929', *Journal of Latin American Studies*, Vol 12, No 2 (1980) pp 342, 343.

5. Hilton, 'Brazil and the Post-Versailles World', pp 347–8; Smith, p 140.
6. Melo, p 122.
7. Hilton, 'Brazil and the Post-Versailles World', p 349; Smith, p 146; Brazilian Foreign Ministry commentary at: http://www2.mre.gov.br/missoes_paz/ing/capitulo6.html
8. Melo, pp 152–7.
9. Melo, pp 152–7.

8: Last Days of the Republic: 1922–30

1. Hilton, *Brazil and the Soviet Challenge 1917–1947*, p 4.
2. Gabaglia, pp 701–8.
3. Quoted at Gabaglia, p 704.
4. Gabaglia, pp 716–18.
5. See Smith, pp 167–82 for detail; Smith, p 168 and p 129; Hilton, 'Brazil and the Post-Versailles World', p 352; Gabaglia, p 751.
6. José Carlos de Macedo Soares, *Brazil and the League of Nations* (Pedone, Paris: 1928) p 136; see also Smith, pp 170–1.
7. Soares, p 143.
8. Lewin, p 382; *Obras Completas*, Vol 24, p 19.
9. This letter is in the Arquivo de Epitácio Pessoa in Rio de Janeiro, and cited by Linda Lewin in 'The Papers of Epitacio Pessoa: An Archival Note and a Personal Comment PII', *Luso-Brazilian Review*, Vol 33, No 1 (Summer 1996) pp 1–20.
10. Gabaglia, pp 898–9.
11. Gabaglia, p 899.

Chronology

YEAR	AGE	THE LIFE AND THE LAND
1865		Epitácio Lindolfo da Silva Pessoa (EP) born at Umbuzeiro in the state of Paraíba, Brazil.
1882	17	EP enters prestigious Recife Law School.
1886	21	EP graduates near the top of his class.
1888	23	Brazil abolishes slave trade.
1889	24	The Brazilian monarchy overthrown and replaced by new Republic. Emperor Pedro II goes into exile. EP in Rio de Janeiro to witness some of the events at first hand.
1890	25	EP becomes federal deputy for home state of Paraíba.
1891	26	First president Deodoro da Fonseca resigns; replaced by another military man, Floriano Peixoto. EP criticises him in Congress.

YEAR	HISTORY	CULTURE
1865	American Civil War ends. Transatlantic telegraph cable completed.	Lewis Carroll, *Alice's Adventures in Wonderland*.
1882	Triple Alliance between Italy, Germany and Austria-Hungary. British occupy Cairo.	R L Stevenson, *Treasure Island*.
1886	Irish Home Rule Bill introduced by Prime Minister Gladstone.	Frances Hodgson Burnett, *Little Lord Fauntleroy*.
1888	Kaiser Wilhelm II accedes to the German throne. Suez Canal convention.	Rudyard Kipling, *Plain Tales from the Hills*.
1889	Austro-Hungarian Crown Prince Rudolf commits suicide at Mayerling. London Dock Strike.	Jerome K Jerome, *Three Men in a Boat*. Richard Strauss, *Don Juan*.
1890	Bismarck dismissed by Wilhelm II.	Oscar Wilde, *The Picture of Dorian Gray*.
1891	Triple Alliance (Austria-Hungary, Germany, Italy) renewed for 12 years. Franco-Russian entente. Young Turk Movement founded in Vienna.	Thomas Hardy, *Tess of the D'Urbervilles*.

YEAR	AGE	THE LIFE AND THE LAND
1894	29	Brazil's first civilian president, Prudente de Morais, takes office. EP, in law practice in Rio, marries Francisca Justiniana das Chagas.
1895	30	Francisca dies in childbirth in Paris; baby dies too.
1897	32	End of Canudos protest in Bahia state.
1898	33	EP marries Maria da Conceição Manso Sayão. Appointed Minister of Justice by new president Manuel Ferraz de Campos Sales.
1899	34	Brazil declines seat at First Hague Conference.
1901	36	EP steps down as Minister of Justice.
1902	37	Baron do Rio Branco becomes Foreign Minister. EP becomes Supreme Court judge and Attorney General.
1905	40	EP steps down as Attorney General.
1907	42	Brazilian politician Rui Barbosa heads delegation to Second Hague Conference

YEAR	HISTORY	CULTURE
1894	Sino-Japanese War begins: Japanese defeat Chinese at Port Arthur.	G & W Grossmith, *The Diary of a Nobody*. Anthony Hope, *The Prisoner of Zenda*.
1895	Sino-Japanese War ends. Cuba rebels against Spanish rule.	H G Wells, *The Time Machine*. Tchaikovsky, *Swan Lake*.
1897	Queen Victoria's Diamond Jubilee. Zionist Congress in Basel, Switzerland.	H G Wells, *The Invisible Man*. Edmond Rostand, *Cyrano de Bergerac*.
1898	Kitchener defeats Mahdists at Omdurman. Spanish-American War: US gains Cuba, Puerto Rico, Guam and the Philippines.	Henry James, *The Turn of the Screw*.
1899	Outbreak of Second Boer War.	Elgar, *Enigma Variations*.
1901	Queen Victoria dies. US President McKinley assassinated: Theodore Roosevelt sworn in as President.	Rudyard Kipling, *Kim*.
1902	Treaty of Vereenigung ends Boer War USA acquires perpetual control over Panama Canal.	Arthur Conan Doyle, *The Hound of the Baskervilles*.
1905	End of Russo-Japanese War.	E M Forster, *Where Angels Fear to Tread*.
1907	Rasputin gains influence at court of Tsar Nicholas II.	Joseph Conrad, *The Secret Agent*.

YEAR	AGE	THE LIFE AND THE LAND
1909	44	EP asked to draw up international public law code.
1910	45	Marshal Hermes da Fonseca becomes first military president in Brazil since 1894.
1912	47	EP finally steps down from Supreme Court due to ill health. Later in same year becomes federal senator for his home state of Paraíba.
1913	48	EP elected head of state party in Paraíba.
1914	49	Brazil declares neutrality after outbreak of war in Europe.
1915	50	As senator, EP helps oversee introduction of new Civil Code he first commissioned as Minister of Justice.
1917	52	26 Oct: Brazil declares war on Germany after sinking of Brazilian merchant shipping.

YEAR	HISTORY	CULTURE
1909	Kiamil Pasha, grand vizier of Turkey, forced to resign by Turkish nationalists.	H G Wells, *Tono-Bungay*.
1910	King Edward VII dies; succeeded by George V. King Manuel II flees Portugal to England. Portugal proclaimed a republic.	E M Forster, *Howard's End*.
1912	*Titanic* sinks. Woodrow Wilson elected US President.	C G Jung, *The Theory of Psychoanalysis*.
1913	US Federal Reserve System established.	D H Lawrence, *Sons and Lovers*.
1914	Archduke Franz Ferdinand of Austria-Hungary and his wife assassinated in Sarajevo. Outbreak of First World War: Battles of Mons, the Marne and First Ypres.	Film: Charlie Chaplin in *Making a Living*.
1915	First World War: Battles of Neuve Chapelle and Loos. Germans sink British liner *Lusitania,* killing 1,198.	Joseph Conrad, *Victory*. Film: *The Birth of a Nation*.
1917	First World War. February Revolution in Russia. USA declares war on Germany.	T S Eliot, *Prufrock and Other Observations*. Film: *Easy Street*.

YEAR	AGE	THE LIFE AND THE LAND
1918	53	Allied powers invite Brazil to be part of Peace Conference; EP named head of the delegation.
1919	54	EP leads Brazilian delegation to Paris.
		Apr: President Rodrigues Alves dies in office; EP unexpectedly named official candidate to replace him; elected President of Brazil while still in Paris.
		Jul: Returns home to take up office after visits to Belgium, Italy, Britain, Portugal, US and Canada.
1922	57	Jul: Junior officers stage brief revolt in Rio.
		EP leads Brazil's celebrations for its centenary of independence. EP's term of office ends.
1923	58	EP appointed judge at Permanent Court of International Justice in The Hague.

YEAR	HISTORY	CULTURE
1918	First World War.	Gerald Manley Hopkins, *Poems*.
	Peace Treaty of Brest-Litovsk between Russia and Central Powers.	
	German Spring offensives on Western Front fail.	
	Allied offensives on Western Front have German army in full retreat.	
	Armistice signed between Allies and Germany.	
1919	Communist Revolt in Berlin.	George Bernard Shaw, *Heartbreak House*.
	Benito Mussolini founds fascist movement in Italy.	Film: *The Cabinet of Dr Caligari*.
	Treaty of Versailles signed.	
	US Senate votes against ratification of Versailles Treaty, leaving the USA outside the League of Nations.	
1922	Chanak crisis.	T S Eliot, *The Waste Land*.
	League of Nations council approves British mandate in Palestine.	British Broadcasting Company (later Corporation) (BBC) founded: first radio broadcasts.
1923	French and Belgian troops occupy Ruhr.	Sigmund Freud, *The Ego and the Id*.
	USSR formally comes into existence.	BBC listings magazine *Radio Times* first published.
	Adolf Hitler's Beer Hall Putsch fails.	

YEAR	AGE	THE LIFE AND THE LAND
1924	59	Second armed revolt by junior officers leads to march of young soldiers known as Prestes Column; EP's book *Pela Verdade* published.
1926	61	Brazil quits League of Nations over admission of Germany.
1929	64	Creation of loosely bound opposition movement known as the Liberal Alliance.
1930	65	Disputed elections over successor to Washington Luís. Failed Liberal Alliance vice-presidential candidate João Pessoa – EP's nephew and friend – murdered in Recife. This and coup in neighbouring Argentina help create revolutionary atmosphere. In October army seizes power and hands presidency to defeated candidate Getúlio Vargas. End of First Republic. Heartbroken, EP resigns as judge at The Hague and retires from political life.
1934	69	New Brazilian constitution approved. Getúlio Vargas voted to continue as president by Constituent Assembly members.

YEAR	HISTORY	CULTURE
1924	Dawes Plan published.	Noel Coward, *The Vortex.*
	Labour Party loses general election after *Daily Mail* publishes Zinoviev Letter.	E M Forster, *A Passage to India.*
	Nazi party enters the German Reichstag with 32 seats for the first time.	
	Calvin Coolidge wins US Presidential Election.	
1926	General Strike in Great Britain.	Ernest Hemingway, *The Sun Also Rises.*
		Film: *The General.*
1929	Germany accepts Young Plan at Reparations Conference in the Hague: Allies agree to evacuate Rhineland.	Erich Remarque, *All Quiet on the Western Front.*
	The Wall Street Crash.	
1930	Britain, France, Italy, Japan and US sign London Naval Treaty regulating naval expansion.	W H Auden, *Poems.*
		Noel Coward, *Private Lives.*
	Nazi party in Germany gains 107 seats.	
	Name of Constantinople changed to Istanbul.	
1934	Hitler becomes *Führer* of Germany.	Robert Graves, *I, Claudius.*
		Film: *David Copperfield.*
	USSR admitted to League of Nations.	
	Japan repudiates Washington treaties of 1922 and 1930.	

YEAR	AGE	THE LIFE AND THE LAND
1936	71	EP makes final trip to Europe, and visits Berlin. EP later diagnosed with Parkinson's Disease.
1937	72	Getúlio Vargas rules as dictator and creates *Estado Novo* (New State).
1939	74	Brazil declares neutrality after outbreak of war in Europe.
1942	76	13 Feb: EP dies at his home in Petrópolis. 22 Aug: Brazil declares war on Germany and Italy after losing five ships to U-boat attacks.

YEAR	HISTORY	CULTURE
1936	German troops occupy Rhineland Outbreak of Spanish Civil War.	Berlin Olympics. Films: *Modern Times. Camille. The Petrified Forest. Things to Come.*
1937	Coronation of George VI. Italy joins German-Japanese Anti-Comintern Pact.	John Steinbeck, *Of Mice and Men.* Film: *A Star is Born.*
1939	Spanish Civil War end. Japanese-Soviet clashes in Manchuria. Nazi-Soviet pact. German invasion of Poland: Britain and France declare war. Soviets invade Finland.	James Joyce, *Finnegan's Wake.* Film: *Gone with the Wind.*
1942	Second World War. Rommel defeated at El Alamein. Dolittle Raid: US bombs Tokyo. US invasion of Guadalcanal.	Albert Camus, *The Outsider.* Film: *Casablanca.*

Further Reading

Brazil

The classic general history of this period by a Brazilian author is José Maria Bello's *A History of Modern Brazil 1889–1964* (Stanford University Press, Stanford: 1966) translated into English by James L Taylor. Despite its idiosyncrasies it remains required reading. *A Concise History of Brazil* (Cambridge University Press, Cambridge: 1999) by another Brazilian academic Boris Fausto, and translated by Arthur Brakel, covers a longer period but nonetheless has a very useful section on the First Republic, as well as an insightful description of how and why it fell apart. It was consciously written for a non-Brazilian audience, which makes it more accessible than some other translated Brazilian works. Fausto is also one of the contributing authors to the scholarly *Brazil, Empire and Republic, 1822–1930* (Cambridge University Press, Cambridge: 1989) edited by Leslie Bethell, which is authoritative but not a light read. The American historian E Bradford Burns's *A History of Brazil* (Columbia University Press, New York: 1993) is recommended as a more readable overview of the story of Brazil from colonial times to the modern era. The same author has also edited *A Documentary*

History of Brazil (Knopf, New York: 1966) which contains analysis of the key documents of the First Republic, as well as other eras. A much briefer and very lively account of modern Brazilian history from the days of empire can be found in *Modern Latin America* (Oxford University Press, Oxford: 1989) edited by Thomas E Skidmore and Peter H Smith.

Specific literature on Brazil's involvement in the First World War and the Paris Peace Conference is, perhaps inevitably, less common. A standard and still very useful account can be found in Percy Alvin Martin's *Latin America and the War* (John Hopkins, Baltimore: 1925) while Joseph Smith's fine *Unequal Giants: Diplomatic Relations Between the United States and Brazil, 1889–1930* (University of Pittsburgh, Pittsburgh: 1991) contains a more modern description of Brazil's relationship with the US during the war. The immediate post-war years are also discussed in Joseph S Tulchin's *The Aftermath of War: World War I and US Policy Toward Latin America* (New York University Press, New York: 1971). Meanwhile, because of its subject matter Frederick C Luebke's *Germans in Brazil* (Louisiana State University Press, Baton Rouge: 1987), which charts the history of the German community in the south of the country, inevitably contains a useful insight into wartime attitudes in Brazil. Another book that touches on the wartime mood in Brazil is Thomas E Skidmore's absorbing *Black into White: Race and Nationality in Brazilian Thought* (Duke University Press, Durham and London: 1993) which is an important and very readable analysis of how Brazilian national identity evolved in this critical period in the country's history.

A much-needed survey of Brazilian foreign policy in the 1920s can be found in the article 'Brazil and the Post-Versailles World: Elite Images and Foreign Policy Strategy, 1919–1929' by Stanley E Hilton in the *Journal of Latin American Studies*,

Vol 12, No 2 (1980). Hilton's *Brazil and the Soviet Challenge 1917–1947* (University of Texas, Austin: 1991) discusses the rise of the Brazilian Communist Party and measures taken in the country to clamp down on potential worker opposition. The economic effects of the First World War on Brazil are also discussed in some detail in Bill Albert's *South America and the First World War: The Impact of the War on Brazil, Argentina, Peru and Chile* (Cambridge University Press, Cambridge: 1988). Brazil's role in the League of Nations and its decision to quit in 1926 can be followed in the interesting if tendentious account by José Carlos de Macedo Soares, *Brazil and the League of Nations* (Pedone, Paris: 1928), written shortly after the events it describes.

On Epitácio Pessoa the longest and probably best biography is the two-volume *Epitácio Pessoa* (José Olympio, São Paulo: 1951) written by his daughter Laurita Pessoa Raja Gabaglia, despite the obvious bias created by their relationship. Not only was she present at some key periods of her father's story – for example in Paris in 1919 – she was also able to draw on correspondence between the pair. Epitácio's many speeches and writings are contained in the 25-volume *Obras completas de Epitácio Pessoa* (Instituto Nacional do Livro, Rio de Janeiro: 1955–65) which like Laurita Pessoa's biography is available only in Portuguese. A much shorter and sometimes critical account of his life in Portuguese can be found in *Epitácio Pessoa: Uma Biografia* (Idéia, João Pessoa: 2005) by Fernando Melo. No English-language biography exists of the former president, though much compelling detail and analysis of his life can be found in Linda Lewin's superlative *Politics and Parantela in Paraíba: A Case Study of Family-Based Oligarchy in Brazil* (Princeton University Press, Princeton: 1987).

An excellent and concise introduction to the Paris Peace Conference is Alan Sharp's *The Versailles Settlement: Peacemaking in Paris, 1919* (Macmillan, London: 1991). A much lengthier account is Margaret MacMillan's compelling *Paris 1919: Six Months that Changed the World* (Random House, New York: 2001), which manages to capture the mood of the city at the time of the conference as well as the negotiations themselves. Lord Riddell's *Intimate Diary of the Peace Conference and After 1918–1923* (Victor Gollancz, London: 1933) is an account of someone who was on the fringes of the Conference, but who was in regular contact with the British delegation, including Lloyd George. An insider's view from an American perspective can be found in *What Really Happened at Paris: The Story of the Peace Conference 1918–1919* (Charles Scribner's, New York: 1921) by Edward Mandell House and Charles Seymour. Excerpts of writings from historians and politicians concerning the Conference and the subsequent Treaty are contained in *The Treaty of Versailles* (Greenhaven Press, San Diego: 2002) edited by Jeff Hay. Analysis of the peace process from an American viewpoint is found in *Woodrow Wilson and the Paris Peace Conference* (D C Heath, Lexington: 1972) edited by N Gordon Levin, Jr. Thomas A Bailey's *Woodrow Wilson and The Lost Peace* (Macmillan, New York: 1944) examines the role of Wilson and also American public opinion.

Picture Sources

The author and publishers wish to express their thanks to the following sources of illustrative material and/or permission to reproduce it. They will make proper acknowledgements in future editions in the event that any omissions have occurred.

Corbis Images: p 122. Getty Images: p vi. Topham Picturepoint: p 74.

Endpapers
The Signing of Peace in the Hall of Mirrors, Versailles, 28th June 1919 by Sir William Orpen (Imperial War Museum: Bridgeman Art Library)
Front row: Dr Johannes Bell (Germany) signing with Herr Hermann Müller leaning over him
Middle row (seated, left to right): General Tasker H Bliss, Col E M House, Mr Henry White, Mr Robert Lansing, President Woodrow Wilson (United States); M Georges Clemenceau (France); Mr David Lloyd George, Mr Andrew Bonar Law, Mr Arthur J Balfour, Viscount Milner, Mr G N Barnes (Great Britain); Prince Saionji (Japan)

Back row (left to right): M Eleftherios Venizelos (Greece);
Dr Afonso Costa (Portugal); Lord Riddell (British Press);
Sir George E Foster (Canada); M Nikola Pašić (Serbia);
M Stephen Pichon (France); Col Sir Maurice Hankey,
Mr Edwin S Montagu (Great Britain); the Maharajah of
Bikaner (India); Signor Vittorio Emanuele Orlando (Italy);
M Paul Hymans (Belgium); General Louis Botha (South
Africa); Mr W M Hughes (Australia)

Jacket images
(Front): Imperial War Museum: akg Images.
(Back): *Peace Conference at the Quai d'Orsay* by Sir William
Orpen (Imperial War Museum: akg Images).
Left to right (seated): Signor Orlando (Italy); Mr Robert
Lansing, President Woodrow Wilson (United States); M
Georges Clemenceau (France); Mr David Lloyd George, Mr
Andrew Bonar Law, Mr Arthur J Balfour (Great Britain);
Left to right (standing): M Paul Hymans (Belgium); Mr
Eleftherios Venizelos (Greece); The Emir Feisal (The
Hashemite Kingdom); Mr W F Massey (New Zealand);
General Jan Smuts (South Africa); Col E M House (United
States); General Louis Botha (South Africa); Prince Saionji
(Japan); Mr W M Hughes (Australia); Sir Robert Borden
(Canada); Mr G N Barnes (Great Britain); M Ignacy
Paderewski (Poland)

Index

NB. All family relationships are to Epitácio Pessoa unless otherwise stated.

UK PUBLICATION: November 2008 to December 2010
CLASSIFICATION: Biography/History/
     International Relations
FORMAT: 198 × 128mm
EXTENT: 208pp
ILLUSTRATIONS: 6 photographs plus 4 maps
TERRITORY: world

Chronology of life in context, full index, bibliography innovative layout
with sidebars

Woodrow Wilson: United States of America by Brian Morton
Friedrich Ebert: Germany by Harry Harmer
Georges Clemenceau: France by David Watson
David Lloyd George: Great Britain by Alan Sharp
Prince Saionji: Japan by Jonathan Clements
Wellington Koo: China by Jonathan Clements
Eleftherios Venizelos: Greece by Andrew Dalby
From the Sultan to Atatürk: Turkey by Andrew Mango
The Hashemites: The Dream of Arabia by Robert McNamara
Chaim Weizmann: The Dream of Zion by Tom Fraser
Piip, Meierovics & Voldemaras: Estonia, Latvia & Lithuania by Charlotte Alston
Ignacy Paderewski: Poland by Anita Prazmowska
Beneš, Masaryk: Czechoslovakia by Peter Neville
Károlyi & Bethlen: Hungary by Bryan Cartledge
Karl Renner: Austria by Jamie Bulloch
Vittorio Orlando: Italy by Spencer Di Scala
Pašić & Trumbić: The Kingdom of Serbs, Croats and Slovenes by Dejan Djokic
Aleksandŭr Stamboliĭski: Bulgaria by R J Crampton
Ion Bratianu: Romania by Keith Hitchin
Paul Hymans: Belgium by Sally Marks
General Smuts: South Africa by Antony Lentin
William Hughes: Australia by Carl Bridge
William Massey: New Zealand by James Watson
Sir Robert Borden: Canada by Martin Thornton
Maharajah of Bikaner: India by Hugh Purcell
Afonso Costa: Portugal by Filipe Ribeiro de Meneses
Epitácio Pessoa: Brazil by Michael Streeter
South America by Michael Streeter
Central America by Michael Streeter
South East Asia by Andrew Dalby
The League of Nations by Ruth Henig
Consequences of Peace: The Versailles Settlement – Aftermath and Legacy
     by Alan Sharp